Stig Jørgensen

ON JUSTICE
AND LAW

AARHUS UNIVERSITY PRESS

ISBN 87 7288 614 5

AARHUS UNIVERSITY PRESS
University of Aarhus
DK-8000 Aarhus C
Fax (+45) 8619 8433

ANSI/NISO
Z39.48-1992

The vignette on the cover shows Maāt, identified by the feather on her head. In Egypt, Maāt was the goddess of truth and justice, symbolised by the feather. In the Kingdom of Death the heart of the dead person was put on one of the two scales and weighed against the feather of justice on the other.

PREFACE

Part 1 of this book speaks in favour of a relational theory of law, arguing that the law has various functions (skills), and that most (current) theories of law elevate one or other of these functions to universal status, thus ignoring other sides of the law in their definitions. It is my thesis that any adequate theory of law must be able to explain all relationships. It must be pluralistic.

An argument will also be made against Alf Ross's theory of law as set out in *On Law and Justice* (1968), which was based on logical empiricism and which must therefore by definition eliminate justice as a non-concept in the science of law, as the term has no "semantic reference", i.e. no existence in the external world. On the basis that language and the external world belong to different categories of logic, the somewhat vague presupposition of this school of thought, that it is possible to give an objective description of the external world, is rejected.

Based on a hermeneutic-anthropological perception of the nature of language as a tool, it is postulated that while it is true that the external world enters into our individual consciousness, its *qualification* in language constitutes an action governed by interests and purposes. This perception of language leads us to the conclusion that a language qualification of external phenomena or events does not constitute an objective description, but an inter-subjective interpretation. Any legal qualification of material presented for evaluation thus constitutes an act of interpretation in light of the relevant legal material. The "interpretation" of legal rules and the "interpretation" of facts are thus integral dialectic processes leading to a decision which must be justified through the logical agreement reached between the particular interpretation and evaluation of the legal material on the one hand and the legal facts on the other.

If this understanding of the relationship between language and the external world and between description and interpretation is adopted, the distinction made by logical empiricism between cognition and evaluation vanishes, and we are allowed to continue the traditional approach of the study of law by interpreting the rules of law in light of their purpose and the actual or hypothetical effects of the various possible interpretations. It is postulated that although the law does not constitute a formally logical and closed system, upheld by a general "basic value" or fundamental norm, it does constitute a political-factual "system", not marked by its logical cohesion, but by its openness, while avoiding as far as possible evident mutual contradictions between decisions made at different places in the "system". Contradiction and arbitrariness are two of the most serious breaches of the attitude called "justice", which attitude constitutes one of the fundamental values of law and morality, namely that like cases must be treated alike. The decisive element in any comparison must be the *criteria* for judging equality.

The general thesis of my book is the claim that any interpretation of the legal system must be based on the political-constitutional system, and that this in turn must be understood in light of the dominant ideology. The individual parts of the legal system must similarly be interpreted on the basis of their own *fundamental principles*, which are expressions of the values on which the various legal institutions and legal areas are based. The purpose of the rules of law is to regulate various aspects of social life. Consequently, they express the purposes of such regulation. Any interpretation of purpose must, however, compete with the interest of *the rule of law*, which is important for the proper functioning of society and its *efficacy*.

Legal argumentation is primarily *rule-oriented* as the rules create obligations which must be fulfilled, but as the rules are purpose-based, the interpretation must also pay due regard to the purpose of the rule. The interpretation must thus be *teleological* and hence forward-looking in order to achieve the most "appropriate" effect (pragmatism). Legal argumentation is thus primarily a backward-looking *normative argumentation*, but it is also teleological and pragmatic. One of the arguments presented by jurisprudence as the goal — or one of the goals — of law and the legal decision is *"justice"*. This argumentation is also backward-looking, but it is not normative in the same manner as a reference to a legal rule. Its character is rather that of an immediate evaluation or a reference to morality.

Logical empiricism rejected arguments containing references to "justice", "equity" or "fairness" as empty and meaningless. Part 2 will argue firstly that no fundamental objection to this type of argument exists, and secondly that these are not unstructured references to morality. On the contrary, a common structure in all of the different perceptions of justice — and there are several — appears to be that they refer to a "concept of equality" in one or other form. For there is more than one concept of equality, although all of these concepts have a common structure which appears to reflect fundamental social needs and hence also fundamental human emotions.

Law and morality have much in common. In terms of history they share the same roots and function. In primitive societies law and morality are identical. Law is seen as divine custom, just as morality is. It was not until the Renaissance, when a positive theory of law was formulated, according to which people make the law themselves, that the schism between law and morality became a reality and the problem of justice arose.

Part 2 will isolate the concept of justice from all other links between morality and law and present a detailed analysis of the structure and function of this concept and of its delimitation *vis à vis* natural law.

CONTENTS

PART 1
Justice and Law

Introduction *12*
Epistemology and the Theory of Law *20*
Interpretation and Description *29*
Alf Ross's Theory *38*
Rules and Principles *46*
Model and Analogy *55*
Pluralis Juris *67*
Judicial Discretion *71*
Natural Law and Justice *75*
Conclusions *82*

PART 2
Justice

Introduction *90*
Concept and History *93*
Justice and Equality *96*
Equality or Arbitrariness *99*
Rule — Principle *101*
Morality and Justice *103*
Conditions of Validity or Function *105*
Pluralism and Legal Principles *109*
Anthropology and Politics *114*
Just War and Positive Law *117*
The Law of Reaction *119*
Justice in Literature *121*
Justice and Duty *123*
Symmetry and Justice *126*

Justice as Process *129*
Competence to Act *133*
The Merits of a Case: Law and Politics *135*
Reasonable and Just *137*
Justice and Natural Law *140*
Abuse of the Law *146*
Priority *148*
Conclusions *149*

References *152*
Index *164*

Part 1

Justice and Law

INTRODUCTION

It is now almost 40 years since the publication of *On Law and Justice* (1958), the main work of Alf Ross (1899-1980). This work was a highly qualified attempt at defending a realist and scientific theory of law based on the most prominent theory of science of its time, the so-called logical positivism or logical empiricism. The basic thesis of logical positivism was that only propositions concerning logical or empirical phenomena can be the object of science. So-called metaphysical propositions or value judgements have no "semantic reference", i.e. no demonstrable reference in reality. Whether a proposition is true or false is determined through a verification procedure according to which the semantic content of the proposition is compared with the external world through the application of special measuring procedures. If the "elements" compared coincide, the proposition is true; if they do not, the proposition is false. If there is no measurable reference to the content of the proposition, the proposition is "meaningless" (nonsense).

Implicit in this theory of science was the assumption that the transformation of reality into language terms was an uncomplicated process, as it would otherwise not be possible to compare a language term with a non-language reality. This "naïve" perception of reality characterised all theories of cognition and science in the early part of this century, after the rejection of all idealist theories which had presumed in various ways that reality was structured "rationally", "logically", or "by language". Instead of analysing the relationship between language and reality in the light of this assumption, most current philosophical theories assumed that people possess a kind of "intuitive" ability to transform the external world directly into language. The German phenomenology called this ability *Wesenschau*, while British analytical philosophy took its basis in the traditional "common sense" or ordinary language use. American pragmatism and Scandinavian realism presumed such a transformation ability, while logical positivism attempted to reduce the problem to a minimum by developing a formal scientific language.

The result for the science of law of this cognitive and scientific theory was, on the one hand, a sharp division between knowledge and value judgements which turned a significant portion of traditional legal dogmatic interpretation into subjective value judgements or political statements. On the other hand, it viewed legal interpretation in the light of hypothetical or actual "facts of law" as an intuitive process retrospectively fitted out with suitable grounds. One consequence of this was that the task of the science of law was reduced to "describing" and systematising legal source materials, i.e. laws and derived formal legal norms, legal usage and customs, while "subsidiary" sources of law, such as "legal dogmatism" and "the nature of the matter" had to be rejected as legal source material.

Any reference to "justice", "equity" or other direct value judgements became especially "unscientific". Instead, it became common to refer to "practicability" on the basis of a general presumption to the effect that "forward-looking" or teleological judgements were more scientific than "backward-looking" normative judgements. The general belief of the time that certain values were more objective than others was part of a general belief that politics could be objective, because it was presumed that the absolutely highest goal of society was the maximisation of material goods, and that "social utility" must therefore rank as the highest value without competition.

As indicated, the greatest weakness of logical positivism and other cognitive and scientific theories of the first half of this century was their faith in the existence of "objective description", which led to the consequences noted here. The hermeneutic philosophy of language has later routed this faith by demonstrating the "intentional" nature of cognition, and hence of description, by pointing to the fact that like all *tools*, our language concepts spring perforce from our personal interests and needs. To the science of law, it is particularly interesting that in principle, "description" becomes an "interpretation" and thus a value judgement, which cannot, however, be purely "individual", as this would make language unsuitable as a means of communication. Language use must be based on "inter-subjective" evaluations, which make it possible to transfer the meaning of a term from sender to addressee. Another important consequence of this insight is the fact that the "criterion of truth" cannot be "monistic" but must be "pluralistic", as it must depend on the circumstances of the *fora* and contexts in which the concepts are used.

Thus it is neither objective nor subjective judgements which determine the language interpretation of the sources of law in the light of hypothetical cases, or the "description" of factual matters subjected to legal "subsumption". It is inter-subjective judgements made by lawyers in accordance with "legal method". The decisive element in judicial decisions and the study of law is thus not the "interpretation" of normative sources of law, but the "description" in language of the "facts" under consideration. In reality this is a dialectic process, as the rules of law must be clarified in relation to "typical situations" and then compared with the circumstances of the case before the legal norm is finally specified and the facts qualified in language which makes it possible to develop a formal deductive "legal consequence". In principle, the study and the application of law use the same methods, although the theoretical study of law concerns itself with hypothetical problems, while the concerns of legal application are factual problems.

This more recent insight into the function of language and the relationship between language and reality will prove of major importance for legal science and thus also for legal usage. The realist theory of law is sound when it assumes that it is possible to make controlled statements of reality, but the theory must be adjusted to bring it into line with recent insights into the nature of language as a tool. The result would be that the process of transformation of reality into language would not be left to an irrational intuition under the cover of objectivity, but would be made rational through knowledge and explication of the purposes and intentions, interests and consequences which govern the real world.

Therefore, if a theory of law is not to become "non-theoretical" and thus void of principle, it must be tied to a theory of knowledge and law which builds on the dominant perception of society and its ideological expression in culture and politics. Only through such a link can the interpretation find a basis and a starting point for its "legal evaluations". Jurisprudence must build on the principles of reality and rationality, on knowledge of the interests and types of problems under consideration, and on the principles, norms and concerns which must enter into the legal evaluations. In the chapters to follow I shall give a more detailed account of the consequences for the theory of cognition, the science and application of law which follow from the philosophy of language noted here. The account will also present my view of how the traditional perception of the study of law and the methods of the application of law may be adjusted.

***

For as long as human beings have been in search of scientific rather than mythological answers to the question of the state of reality, they have sought "The immutable in the mutable" (*apeiron*). Since the Ionic natural philosophy of about 500 BC, the basic principles have been the object of the search (Anaximander, 610-547 BC). Later, the search was extended to principles and concepts capable of uniting experience with thought and language. Myth has it that Pythagoras (578-510 BC) sacrificed 200 oxen to the gods when he succeeded in uniting figures with geographical expanse through the Pythagorean theorem.

Plato (427-347 BC) distinguished between ideas as representing the "true" abstract reality, and experience, which was merely imperfect actual instances or representations of true reality, but it was not until Aristotle (384-322 BC) that scientific knowledge and its relation to reality was systematised in a general theory of science. Aristotle distinguished between two forms of analysis, *analytica priori* and *analytica posteriori*. In the former type, which we call logic, he presents a method for drawing absolute deductions from clear premises by applying a set of rules or syllogisms. The syllogism can be used both for analysing the consequences of hypothetical premises, which involves *apodeictic* deductions, where the conclusion is found on the basis of two clear premises; and for analysing the basis of a given assumption, which involves a *dialectic* process by which a premise is found on the basis of another premise and a deduction.

Within the given premises, the deductions are certain, but the fundamental principles must be stipulated through a non-logical mental process, which Aristotle derives from a mental ability called *nous*, and which translates approximately into intuitive intelligence. In *analytica posteriori*, Aristotle discusses the problem of reality and how to insert assumptions about reality as premises in the syllogism, and despite some lack of clarity, it is likely that Aristotle was aware of the inductive nature of knowledge and the importance of intuition for the qualification in language of empirical knowledge. The uncertain element is the question of how one obtains one's premises based on the "external world"; the certain element is the deductions drawn from one's premises, once they have been formulated in concepts defined and delimited in accordance with the rules of *Catagoria*. In *Topica*, Aristotle gives an account of the other categories under which a problem may be qualified, e.g. genus versus species, significant versus insignificant. One important sentence states that what is found under species by necessity will be found in genus, but not *vice versa*. If we have settled that a thing is "red", we may draw the incontrovertible deduction that it is "coloured", but we cannot, from the concept "coloured", derive the colour "red". This premise must depend on material and not logical considerations, and this dependency is an expression of the central problem of qualification in all language processing of the external world. Once this qualification has been performed, the construction of both inductive and deductive statements within a hierarchical genus versus species relational system is a simple matter.

In *Topica*, Aristotle focused mainly on how to draw incontrovertible deductions from premises which are not absolute, but the expression of common views on a given topic where absolute premises are difficult to obtain, especially within morality and politics. The uncertain element is where we obtain our premises from, the certain element is the deductions we draw from them. In his *Rhetorica*, Aristotle lists various categories of arguments which may be used in political discussions and legal proceedings: arguments *ad hominem*, objective arguments, arguments on norms and consequences etc.

In the 1600s, when philosophy tore itself loose from the Scholastic concept of science, it became clear that a dilemma existed, which Descartes (1596-1650) attempted to solve by taking a rational stand, i.e. by upholding absolute knowledge while limiting himself to the world of thought. The problem with this, however, is that there is no certainty that the knowledge is true. This is achieved by empiricism, which involves inductive conclusions based on experience, but at the cost of certainty. During the 19th century, attempts were made to unite the divided categories through idealistic cognitive theories, which solved the dilemma of language qualification by removing it. These theories claimed that reality was structured in language and according to reason, thus enabling direct insight into reality, either as a projection of consciousness into reality, or as a reflection of the rational and logical structure of reality, in German called *Natur der Sache, sachlogische Strukturen*. With the collapse of idealism around the turn of the century, the dilemma of qualification reappeared.

One of the ways to solve the dilemma was through the hermeneutic philosophy of language, which stressed the functional and intentional nature of language and had the power in one sweep to reject both the objective and intuitive "description". For any theory of legal interpretation it is important to stress the link to the rhetorical and hermeneutic theory of exegesis, as revived by Wilhelm Dilthey (1833-1911). The major theses or *canones* of hermeneutics and legal interpretation are analogous: (1) the autonomy of the object of interpretation, by which is understood that the text carries its own message prior to interpretation. (2) the indivisibility of the object, by which is understood that any understanding of the parts must proceed from an understanding of the whole. (3) the origin of the object, which covers a) its subjective teleology, and b) its objective teleology or its author's, the lawmaker's, subjective will on the one hand, and the objective meaning of the text on the other. With regard to the second element, it is important that language has a "generative" meaning, as it always contains an element of "redundancy" due to the open-ended nature of language concepts. The "meaning" of a word or text is thus not what it "means", but what it "may mean". The text may therefore be applied to cases occurring later and which nobody had predicted at the time when the law was drawn up. Finally, one may use (4) the comparative canon, which prescribes a comparison with other texts by the same author, i.e. the systematic relationship between various parts of a law and between various laws.

Legal interpretation cannot, however, satisfy itself with these four canons. The rhetorical figures: analogy or comparison versus contrast, general versus specific, older versus more recent, higher versus lower, and the various attitudes and arguments must also enter into a dialectic process. The decisive issue for us, however, is the general theoretical problem of science that reality must be transformed into language for "knowledge" to be processed in a scientific manner, and so that we can make scientific and practical decisions by a combination partly of a typological interpretation of a system of rules and partly by a qualification in language of a factual event under consideration.

If a language is to play an essential role as a system of social communication, it must be able to contain true information about "reality". If the accordance between language and facts was only accidental, it would be impossible to have any confidence in language information, and hence any predictability, and any organised collaboration based on language would be impossible.

We have presumed that language is a biologically conditioned competence which has developed as a tool to serve people's social needs. We have also assumed that language is structured in a way which shows that its use is more than just a learned process, as rules of grammar and syntax as well as context lend the sequencing of words, their form and their internal relations a special meaning such that a limited number of words can contain unlimited meanings.

There is therefore also reason for believing that it is the same biological selection process through which language has developed, which also conditions it to render a "true" representation of reality. This is how other senses function in a manner essential for the survival of the species and the individual. The sense of sight would, for example, be useless unless one can trust that there is a glass of water where it appears to be when one is thirsty. Mirages constitute useless and dangerous hallucinations.

Although we assume that language and its ability to represent the external world is a result of a biological development process, this does not imply that the use of language is a purely "intuitive" process which cannot be made the object of subsequent rational analysis. Human beings are also rational beings, whose actions are subject to rational control. To a very large extent it is possible within the limits of our total sensory apparatus subsequently to analyse the strategy which led to an action, including a language formulation.

Like all human activities from the most elementary to the most refined, the factual motivational process, the outcome of which is a language expression, constitutes a combination of predispositions and learned reflexes. As will be seen in our analysis of the judicial decision, the motivational process is largely the result of a spontaneous application of an acquired professional legal method. On the other hand, it is — and must be — open for subsequent legal analysis and justification, through which it acquires the character of a judicial decision. In the same manner, spontaneous language application must be able to be made the object of subsequent analysis and justification in terms of the language used.

EPISTEMOLOGY AND THE THEORY OF LAW

In the post-war period, the theory of law was strongly influenced by the general trend of the period towards de-idealisation.

In Germany, the reevaluation of totalitarian political systems led to a return to concepts of natural law based on the view that it had been the positivist perception of law with its identification of justice and state which had been responsible for the "abuse of justice" committed by the Third Reich. The violation of the security of the life and property of individual citizens made possible by the Enabling Act, which permitted the *Führer* to act outside the system and to waive the rules of law, were ascribed by some writers to the strict division of law and morals which had formed the ideal of the so-called "pure theory of law".

This theory of law was an offshoot of the "logical positivism" which had grown into a general theory of science in the cultural environment of Vienna in the period between the two world wars. Its purpose had been to rid science of value judgements in order to make it the object of exact quantitative descriptions capable of forming a solid basis on which to make predictions. Only two types of propositions were therefore permitted in science. They were propositions pertaining to objects in physical reality, which were capable of "verification" or "refutation" through "objective" control methods (synthetic assertions), and propositions covering logical meaning complexes, such as mathematical statements (analytical propositions). Metaphysical propositions on matters lying outside the control and evaluation of the external world lacked "semantic reference" because there was "nothing" in the external world corresponding to the linguistic content of such propositions.

The criterion of truth applied by logical positivism to synthetic propositions was thus the direct correspondence between the words of the proposition, e.g. that the temperature of the air is 20°C, and the objective result of measuring, the reading on a thermometer. In linguistics, the branch of studies concerned with meaning is called "semantics". The term is derived from the Greek word for "sign", and the concept "semantic reference" therefore has meaning only within a theory of language and science based on an identification of "language" and "measuring result" such as are found in logical positivism or scientific empiricism. Logical positivism builds on the premise that it is possible to measure reality "objectively", or that science is limited to the "results of measuring".

This premise links logical positivism to traditional rationalistic and idealistic theories which presume that reality is "rational", or that science must limit itself to what is "rational", i.e., the concept or idea of reality. Both Plato and Aristotle proceeded on the basis that "reality" was the outcome of some eternal principles which science must seek in the kaleidoscope of the empirical world. Plato called these principles "ideas", while Aristotle spoke of the "essence" of things, i.e. the essential attributes serving to identify an object and to lead objects to "strive" to reach a certain state.

Classical epistemology was thus "teleological" in the sense that it assumed that everything had an end or final cause which it strived to realise. This was a view well-suited to the "theological" or scholastic science of the Medieval period, which held that the will of God was the prime mover of all things, and to know the will of God was therefore the object of philosophy.

The nominalistic epistemology of the 1300s, represented by William of Ockham (c. 1290-1349), rejected the Aristotelian proposition that concepts are attributes attached to objects and claimed that concepts are names given to objects: hence "nominalism". By this step, epistemology was released from speculations regarding the final cause of things and allowed instead to turn its attention towards observation of reality (empiricism) or the conception of the external world (rationalism). Ockham's own choice was a form of intuitive empiricism based on his belief that universal concepts could be formed by observation of isolated phenomena. This view illustrates both the inherent strength and weakness of empiricism. It may well be "true" in so far as it concerns itself with the external world, but "uncertain" in so far as it bases its formation of universal concepts or rules on intuitive induction from single cases.

Descartes therefore took the opposite road, basing his theory in thought, this being the only "absolute" left where everything else was open to doubt. Not only the existence of God but also one's own existence could be brought into doubt. The existence of human thought, however, could not be doubted. It was therefore the proof of existence (*cogito ergo sum*), and the thought of God was a sign of the existence of God. The weakness of Descartes' view is the absence of certainty that it is true. Its strength is the certainty with which deductive conclusions may be drawn from the axioms on which the thought is based.

During the 18th century, this rationalism was further elaborated and given a mathematical precision which empowered science to handle complicated data with precision and speed. It was exactly the fact that concepts had been emptied of all material content and reduced to pure form which made possible the construction of a universal tool, but on the other hand no more than a tool, for the processing of data, not of reality *per se*.

In the late 1700s this rationalist epistemology broke down in the face of the Scot David Hume's (1711-76) fundamental criticism of epistemology. His thesis was not entirely new. It stated that no generalisation can be made inductively from any single observation with any certainty, but only "intuitively". It follows, therefore, that we cannot prove causation any more than we can prove that values are attributes attached to objects, as Classical, Medieval and Rationalist ethics had assumed. "Good" and "evil" are thus not attributes attached to things but an expression of the feelings of the observer.

While recognising the truth of Hume's criticism, the German philosopher Immanuel Kant (1724-1804) came to a different conclusion by stipulating that human beings have to "assume" certain necessary conditions of cognition. He found these conditions in the human cognitive faculties in the broadest sense, the senses and the brain, which processes the impressions of reality formed by the senses.

Kant divided knowledge into "theoretical" and "practical" portions. The former deals with the external world which may only be "understood" if, among other conditions, we assume the existence of causation. If this assumption is not made, reality would collapse into a chaotic heap of events incapable of explanation or prediction. It is essential for us to "understand" in this sense, because human beings are "rational beings" in contrast to "natural beings", and to do so, we must assume the existence of causation.

When, on the other hand, the issue is human actions, we must assume the existence of free will. Otherwise it would be impossible to apply the concept of "responsibility", which only applies when human beings have freedom of choice. Kant therefore agrees with Hume in the latter's rejection of the rationalists' theory of natural law, which had asserted that an "objective" morality existed, based on the insight of reason into human nature, which was presumed to be eternal and immutable. It is true that it is not "humanity" which thinks and feels, but individual human beings, and thus no basis exists for a material morality applicable to all human beings at all times.

Kant does not hold, however, that every objective morality must be rejected, as it is possible to formulate some fundamental moral principles by logical deduction from some general principles. The basic postulate used by Kant is the assumption that as rational beings, all humans possess freedom of will as noted above. Further, that thus formulated universally, the postulate implies that all humans' free will must respect the similar free will of other human beings in accordance with positive statutes given by the state. It is worth noting that the state was then in the process of emerging as a European form of organisation. The period of revolutions and Napoleon's reign was an expression precisely of the dynamic social development which had followed on the heels of the industrial revolution and which found its ideological legitimation in the nation and its history.

The "idealism" developed on the basis of Kant's conditions of cognition limited science to that part of reality which our sensory apparatus and cognitive faculties were capable of processing. Romantic philosophy which separated the I from the non-I drew the conclusion from this that it is the individual human beings who "project" their ideas on to the surrounding world, thus constituting it. G.W.F. Hegel (1770-1831) took the opposite view, that reality is already logically constituted and that consequently, it is "reflected" in human consciousness: "What is real is rational and what is rational is real".

Idealistic epistemology dominated the 19th century, and in a sense it rendered knowledge unproblematic, as it presupposed a correspondence between the cognitive faculties of the human being and the external world, which was perceived either as a projection of the ideas of the individual human being, or as a reflection of logical structures. Description in language was therefore an uncomplicated logical process.

This idealism was to collapse simultaneously in several places around the turn of the century. From its ruins, a new division between reality and language emerged, and various attempts at breaching the gap were made. In England G.E. Moore (1873-1958) rejected the idea that reality is logical in nature or a projection of the subjective consciousness. Moore assumed that the "objective" reality as such is a direct part of consciousness and is translated into language by the means of *common sense*. Moore similarly assumed that no logical connection exists between fact and duty within ethics, and that therefore no "ought" could ever be deduced from an "is". He rejected both naturalistic and utilitarian grounds for morality. But rather than assuming a subjective theory of duty as a consequence of this, he maintained that values have an objective nature into which individual human beings may gain insight through intuition. A close link thus exists between common sense in epistemology and intuition in ethics, in the sense that attempts are made to reestablish the language link between consciousness and reality through intuition.

Intuition was similarly the tool of Henri Bergson (1859-1941) in his dismissal of idealism. Like Moore, he assumed that human consciousness has an "objective" structure which enables us to perceive the external world directly through intuition. On the other hand, and like J.G. Fichte (1762-1814), he also assumed that all philosophy is tied to the basic starting point chosen by the individual philosopher. "*Wesenschau*" was the name given to this view in the phenomenological philosophy based on it and developed mainly by Edmund Husserl (1859-1938). Husserl was, however, also influenced by Franz v. Brentano, who partly rejected any link between logical and physical reality and who partly revived the Classical and Scholastic distinction between essential and non-essential attributes as well as "intentionality" of thought.

Like Romantic philosophy, intuitivism was based on the assumption of a fundamental distinction between the "I" and the "non-I", but with the difference that while the subjective idealism (Romanticism) saw the external world as constituted by the subjective consciousness, British, French and German intuitivism "believed" in the external world. In contrast to the "objective idealism" of Hegel, however, they also rejected the logical structure of the external world and hence its "language" character. Instead, they saw the "objective" reality enter into the "subjective" consciousness by means of an intuitive mechanism which escapes scientific control. "Common sense" is the tool used in British theory, while "*Wesenschau*" is similarly used in German theory.

In North America, "pragmatist" philosophers such as William James (1842-1910) took a different road, redefining instead the concept of truth. The decisive factor in knowledge was not truth but usefulness. The problem facing a pragmatic epistemology which retains its belief in the existence of the external world is to decide when an action is "useful". Like the "intentionalism" of phenomenology, pragmatism assumes "instrumentalism" as a general supra-individual yardstick or consensus, which it is difficult to establish objectively.

Accepting the consequences of this uncertainty, "Scandinavian realism" rejected all thoughts of scientific treatment of "metaphysical" phenomena and values. According to Axel Hägerström (1868-1939), science can only be concerned with the physical reality which exists in the sense that it allows itself to be fitted into the time and space of a "world of experience", while being capable of description, interpretation and systematisation through observation and induction. As metaphysical phenomena and values do not belong in this world of experience, they escape objective and scientific investigation, but enter into the subjective consciousness. As noted above, this logical positivism is not a theory of cognition, but a theory of science which limits the task of science to propositions about "verifiable" phenomena. Turning to ethics and the philosophy of law, the result is the same as for "Scandinavian realism", namely that metaphysical and value judgements become "meaningless" because they have no "semantic reference", i.e. there is no yardstick by which to measure their correspondence with the semantic content of the proposition.

Neither Scandinavian realism nor logical positivism offers any clear suggestion as to the relationship between language and reality, although the existence of reality is assumed. While logical positivism attempts through language analysis to develop an exact scientific language postulated to offer a one-to-one correspondence with the phenomena under scrutiny, Scandinavian realism takes its point of departure in daily language use. The world of experience, which is an important concept, is closely related to the older L. Wittgenstein's (1889-1951) and Martin Heidegger's (1889-1976) "Lebenswelt" and thus to the hermeneutic theory of language, but in its unanalysed form it had more in common with the intuitive common sense theory.

We have returned to our starting point: post-war philosophy and science felt a need to distance itself from the ideologies which had been identified with the totalitarian ideologies. It is understandable, therefore, that logical positivism won a strong position, having been developed, as it were, partly with this purpose in mind, partly as a reflection of a scepticism based on wartime experiences, and partly because of its suitability as the philosophy of a period marked by its general consensus that the goal of post-war policy was the rebuilding of Europe. It is therefore understandable that leading politicians could be heard expressing their views on "impartial" politics in contrast to "partial" politics. American pragmatism similarly stressed "suitability of purpose" as a criterion of correct action in contrast to "justice" or "rightness".

The British common sense philosophy likewise took its basis in factual conditions and factual decisions which decided unambiguously what was the right knowledge and the right action. "Ordinary language use" could legitimise a decision based on intuition without it being considered a problem that this made it impossible to check the decision by rational means.

Where the philosophy of law is concerned, the total result of "American realism", British "analytical philosophy", "Scandinavian realism" and "logical positivism" was that it was the actual judicial decisions which became the criterion for determining what was applicable or "valid" law in society. Any criticism of the judicial decision loses its meaning, and the one task left to the philosophy of law is in principle merely the listing and systematising of laws along with derived sources and judicial decisions.

When, in contrast, German lawyers sought to revive the traditional natural law theory, they were motivated by the belief that the positivist theory of law carried the main responsibility for the success of Nazism, as lawyers of the Third Reich must see the law as a tool of the State and themselves as impartial administrators of the State's rules of law. Legal positivism does not recognise any "right of reaction" against unjust laws or laws which "violate natural rights". Law and morality belong in different categories.

This claim may well be questioned, however, as the "assumption of power" took place in accordance with the Weimar Constitution and the results of the "*Führer* system" only appeared gradually. To this should be added the fact that putting their training and administrative functions to use, lawyers long delayed and prevented the worst abuses which therefore had to be left to special "people's courts". More serious is the criticism which has been levelled against the German post-war natural law theories to the effect that by rejecting a "rationalist" and "positivist" theory in favour of another irrational theory, they indirectly legitimise former Nazi tendencies. Like Romantic and historical philosophy of law, Nazi jurisprudence rejected reason as the source of law, and just as the former took its basis in the "human spirit", Nazism found its authority in the "community of race". "*Treu und Glauben*" in *Bundesgesetzbuch* Section 242 was, readily and without alteration, a sentence of the law reinterpreted as "*gesundes Volksempfinden*".

Neither is it only neo-natural law theories whose irrational basis exposes them to criticism. More recent theories which focus on "discourse" (Jürgen Habermas) and "institutions" seek their basis in similar fictitious concepts such as the "social contract" (Grotius, J. Rawls), for example, or "*faktische Verhältnisse*", "*Rechtsverhältnisse*" and other "institutions" (O. Weinberger, N. MacCormick).

The anti-ideological theory of science formulated in the 60s was a dubious theory because it was in fundamental opposition to the ethical principle of science, that the expressions of opinion of others should be taken at face value until the opposite is proved likely through sound reasoning. One of the fathers of this school, Th. Adorno (1903-69), turned against its excesses in his comment on "argumentative" critics who demanded a maximum of arguments for self-evident truths and a minimum of arguments for their own provocational criticism and expressions of opinion.

No criticism of science and society, unless based on an expert command of an existing science or the existing social order and a set of well-founded arguments in favour of another theory or another social order, constitutes a critique, but is merely an expression of dissatisfaction. And indeed, the anti-ideological theory of science has later been called the "hermeneutics of suspicion", and its "liberating" function has been called into doubt as experiences from the dissolution of Eastern Europe have given the lie to the ability of Marxism to lend the citizens of these countries a sense of freedom.

This is not to say that science should not be critical: only that scientific theory may not come into apparent conflict with scientific ethics. As noted below, the politics of law are also part of the science of law, but in principle the practical, "dogmatic" science of law cannot be critical in the sense that it contains good advice to the legislature camouflaged as statements about the current state of law, *de lege ferenda*. It is, however, a permissible — even necessary — part of legal dogmatics to express one's well-founded "interpretations" of valid law in the form of well-founded advice to those responsible for the application of the law, to the effect of determining which of several possible solutions should be preferred based on proper weighing of purpose, consequences and other legal considerations, *de sententia ferenda*.

INTERPRETATION AND DESCRIPTION

The main weakness of the various epistemologies discussed in the previous chapter was their failure to explain the connection between language and reality. An idealist theory assumes that reality is either a projection of the human consciousness or a rational — logical — structure capable of direct reflection in the human consciousness. A realist theory assumes an intuitive mechanism which transforms objective physical reality directly — subconsciously — into consciousness (*Wesenschau*, common sense). Logical positivism attempts to avoid the problem by reducing language to a formal system of scientific notation (figures and symbols).

The various theories did, however, contain elements pointing forwards towards a clearer understanding of the independent and creative nature of language. In association with Fichte's subjective idealism, phenomenology had already stressed the *intentionality* of language, i.e. its instrumental character. Heidegger also sought inspiration in Dilthey's *hermeneutics*, stressing the function of language as a *message* which carries meaning only within a set temporal and conceptual framework. Only people who are familiar with this framework and with the function of the phenomenon are able to *understand* the message. Thus, all language terms and all messages must be *interpreted* on the basis of such conceptual systems, the product of history and human conditions. From this arises the hermeneutic circle, which asserts that we cannot understand the individual parts without knowing the whole, and we cannot understand the whole without knowing the individual parts. Understanding thus becomes a dialectic process between contemplation of individual parts and the whole.

Both British analytical philosophy and Scandinavian realism contained elements of such common hermeneutics. Wittgenstein, who originally belonged to the Vienna circle of logical positivists, became influenced by the common sense philosophy of G.E. Moore and Bertrand Russell (1872-1970) during his visit to England, and gave up the idea that language was a picture of reality due to a common logical structure. He developed a new theory related to the hermeneutic, in so far as he saw language as a tool which assumes its importance relative to various circumstances and various purposes ("form of life"), a theory which J.L. Austin (1911-60) was to develop further ("how to do things with words").

Hägerström also felt that the external world must be described in relation to a system of principles, but his theory of the description of reality was less clear, as he kept within ordinary language use, as the British common sense philosophy had done. Alf Ross, on the other hand, adopted the approach of logical positivism and its theory of the shared logical structure of reality and language, which makes objective description (semantic reference) possible. While from the perspective of natural sciences the claim that reality may be objectively described in a formalised scientific notation may not seem particularly problematic, it does become problematic when applied to texts written in normal language, or to the description of facts relative to such a normal language. It is especially applicable to the legal function that whether its task is a dogmatic description of a normative system or the application of a normative system to practical legal decisions, both administrative and judicial, the central issue is the qualification of a factual event relative to an abstract normative system, or in other words, how to give an abstract normative system concrete form in relation to an actual event.

It is thus not possible to separate the interpretation of norms from the qualification of facts, and the greatest difficulty is not the interpretation of legal source material, once selected from the total material, but to qualify the actual event. When this interpretation of legal source material has reached its conclusion in the pinpointing of the exact rule, and the factual event has been qualified relative to this rule, it is a matter of simple *deduction* to draw the consequences in law. But the judicial decision *as such*, that is to say in the external world, is not a logical but a psychological process consisting of a string of value judgements, on the outcome of which a stand is taken on which parts of the normative system may apply, how these should be ranked, and how the language terms should be interpreted with due regard to the purpose of the normative material. Then, or proceeding dialectically, the relevant facts must be selected from the factual circumstances and qualified relative to the normative material.

While the task of legal dogmatics is to describe and interpret the normative material in a systematic fashion, the task of the judicial decision is to determine which legal consequences should apply to a fact or a factual process. But in principle in both cases the task is to decide which hypothetical or factual single cases should release certain legal consequences.

The interpretation or significance of language terms may depend on the *purpose* of the term. There is therefore a difference between the interpretation of literary and authoritative texts. Literary interpretation must take its basis in the consciousness of the addressee, as the purpose of art is to evoke an experience of art. In contrast, the interpretation of authoritative texts must take its basis in the authority's intentions in using the terms, as the *purpose* of the text is to cause certain effects to occur. Theology and law have in common that their main task is to determine in which cases the authoritative text authorises certain consequences. Where rules of law are concerned this purpose is to influence social behaviour by linking certain legal consequences to compliance with or deviation from that which was intended.

The interpretation of law must therefore contain both *teleological* and *pragmatic* elements; and, in societies governed by law at any rate, its basis must be "common language use", because the *rule of law* requires that individual people must be able to predict and calculate the consequences of their actions. This would not be possible if the verbal message of the rules had no "objective" content of any kind. Communication of language content can only succeed if the sender and the addressee surround the content of the message with the same kind of consciousness. Language does not, however, possess any such objective significance, but it is possible to operate with an "inter-subjective" significance or several "intersubjective" significances depending on the "conceptual horizon", the "forum" or the "environment" to which the subjects belong.

Where clarification is the aim of interpretation, it is, however, necessary also to consider the purpose of the rules, that is to say the social effects which the rules are intended to have, and in the event of several possible interpretations, the extent to which the various effects will satisfy the established purpose and considerations of law and order (factual considerations).

The purpose of laws is no longer as clear as in the ordinances of former days, when a "preamble" often expressed the intentions of the sovereign in general terms. With the parliamentary legislation of anonymous democracies, the purpose was not expressed in the text as such, but in the preliminary work. The purpose is not, however, part of the rule to such an extent that it may not be realised within the ordinary word limits, unless the law itself defines certain concepts in a special way, or if an analogy or extensive interpretation may be required.

To ensure the security of life and property, conclusions by analogy are normally prohibited in criminal law, except in cases of "complete analogy", and if the purpose would otherwise be lost. Normally, this will also apply to tax law and general administrative law where interpretations are involved which may cause harm to citizens. Earlier this century, when the "welfare state" was still seen as a positive factor, there was a greater tendency to accept without reflection the indication of purpose given in the preliminary texts of an administrative law and its consequent administrative practice. More recently, with the growth of the public sector, the state is no longer seen as a benefactor whose good intentions must be carried out at the cost of law and order, but as a mighty adversary whose power must be restricted as far as possible. This development explains both the increasing tendency of judicial decisions to refer to the preliminary texts of laws and to administrative practice, and the equally increasing tendency to place distance to the latter unless they show a plain and clear correspondence with the words of the law.

Within traditional private law a greater need exists, however, for analogical and elaborate interpretations as a greater degree of adaptation to practical needs and social development is required, and as considerations of law and order are less important than the "factual considerations", that is the average interests of the parties. And indeed it is within private law that customary law, or common law, has found its importance as a source of law. In pre-state societies, custom is the only source of law, and private law is there the absolute dominant factor, as both the right of redress and the legal system formed part of private law, inasmuch as legal proceedings in general are a private matter.

In a legal system applying natural and idealistic law, justice is a basic principle and equity a self-evident requirement of the application of law. In contrast, within positivist and especially realist theories of law, such arguments are not permissible. They are therefore replaced by such utilitarian terms as "practical" or "factual reasons would dictate" etc., unless resort is taken to general references to "social utility" or the "demands of life" etc. It is obvious that no action can be more or less practical unless in relation to a particular purpose, and that no "factual considerations" mean anything without realities. As Alf Ross has pointed out in his criticism of Vilh. Lundstedt (1882-1955) and F. Vinding Kruse (1880-1963), terms such as "social utility" and the "demands of life" can justify anything, and are in reality a hidden reference to that justice or equity which, when turned out at the front door, crept back in at the back.

In the same way, without further account of the values of the speaker, references to practicality and factual considerations constitute just such hidden or suppressed references to direct values as equity and justice. It is interesting to note that in cases concerning administrative law, more recent legal practice is beginning increasingly to use this type of argument while at the same time taking a critical stance against utilitarian arguments in favour of law and order.

While difficulties are thus encountered in the selection and interpretation of the authoritative legal source material before a particular rule of law can be pinpointed, even greater problems are connected with the language qualification of the facts presented for judgement. From among such facts, the legally relevant or significant facts must first be selected, that is the facts which are significant for the formulation of a general rule, in contrast to circumstances which have no significance for the formulation of the abstract rule to be applied. In the selection of such facts, it is of course of crucial importance which rule or rules may be applied.

If this is a penal rule, any financial loss will be of less importance, whereas it will be of primary importance in an action for damages. Facts relating to the behaviour shown will, however, be relevant in the application of both a penal rule and a rule of torts (*culpa*, intent, negligence).

In the description of the data selected, it must be remembered that such "raw facts" cannot enter into a person's language processing consciousness without themselves being transformed into language. If using one of the above "intuitive" cognitive theories or the common sense theories, one risks suppressing those values which enter into the language qualification of "facts" and unwittingly continue the "jurisprudence of concepts" of earlier times.

"Jurisprudence of concepts" is the derogatory term given by Rudolph v. Jhering (1818-92) to the German constructive jurisprudence of the early 19th century. Its purpose was, in the interest of law and order, to construct a coherent system of general legal concepts aimed at providing an exhaustive and non-contradictory account of the legal system. Its advantage was certainty in application, which was believed to be based on simple logical deductions and, in case of doubt, on an elaboration of the concepts instead of a weighing up of practical considerations.

As indicated, its weakness was the same as had marred the earlier rationalism, namely that its certainty was balanced by an equal absence of truth, that is to say accordance with the practical purpose of the rules. The fact was that "the law of concepts" had adopted the assumption underpinning all rationalism, both the rationalist natural law theory as well as its precursors in the scholastic ethics, which had in turn been based on Aristotle's metaphysics. The basic thesis of these theories had been that the same fundamental principles which constitute the nature of things and actions also determine their consequences. As reason is the nature of human beings, it is also rational expectations which should determine the legal and moral consequences of human actions in all matters.

These "rationalist" principles pervade any system which fails to recognise the instrumental nature of language and fails as well to account for and take into account the practical problems which it is the object of the political-legal systems to solve. Certainty is thus gained at the cost of practical applicability. The idea that legal solutions occur as the result of a logical process of "deduction" is linked with the epistemological perception of the logical structure of reality.

An echo of this rationalism is the still prevalent tendency to derive the consequences and their limitations in private law from the facts forming the legal basis. In contract law, attempts have been made to establish the limitations of declarations of intention in the parties' "prior conditions", just as the limitations of liability for the consequences of tortious acts are sought in "foreseeability". By doing so one evades the very complicated practical evaluations regarding the extent of the legal effects which enter into these intuitively made decisions, whether such decisions are derived from the "doctrine of prior conditions" or from the "concept of causation" in accordance with "common sense".

In British legal usage, the dilemma has been most evidently expressed in the contradictory judgements on "remoteness of damages" of the House of Lords (Richard Kidnar in *Legal Studies*, 1989, p. 1). In the older *Re Polemis*, the House of Lords assumed that *direct* damages were covered by liability whether foreseeable or not. Later in *Waggon Mound*, the Upper House assumed that notwithstanding the above, foreseeability was the decisive criterion; however, later legal usage has paradoxically established that foreseeability does not carry the same meaning in cases of damage to persons — where the concept is stretched more widely — as in cases of damage to property. The same distinction is made in other countries, undoubtedly from considerations of providing greater protection for personal integrity than for property. It is, however, a distortion of facts to suppress this value judgement and instead maintain a rationalist but empty criterion.

The principal basis of jurisprudence of concepts is, however, correct. It is true that every new experience gained is "understood" by giving it a name and thus incorporating it into our language and conceptual system. When a child is born, the parents do not say "Look, there's Peter!" The child is given a name. We also name things according to those of our previous experiences which they most *resemble*. The expansion of our experience thus does not follow a logical but an *analogical* process, by which we determine on the basis of our experiences which former conceptually defined experiences we choose to assign them to. Concepts in our daily language are not clearly defined general concepts determined by precisely limited and stated elements, but *concepts of types*, which are less clearly defined and more closely determined by the intensity of the elements than by their internal relations. They are therefore open to new experiences and they are open-ended, so that it cannot be determined beforehand which things and situations they cover.

It follows from the hermeneutic language theory that our concepts are "intentional" (determined by interest) and are ascribed their significance within an individual or "intersubjective" system of ideas, an ideology in the broadest sense. We thus introduce our interests and values into our use of concepts causing the latter to reflect the "value system" which we have each built into our separate consciousnesses. Through their professional training, lawyers have an in-built doctrine and method, the legal method, which, in contrast to non-lawyers, predisposes them to make decisions on the basis of a generalising tendency, taking account not only of the circumstances of the actual situation but also of the need to reach a decision which may serve as a model for future decisions. Lawyers thus react intuitively out of consideration for law and order and formal justice in the same way as art lovers and tradesmen react spontaneously on the basis of the tasks which they have been trained to solve.

As Knud Illum (1906-83) put it, it is therefore no more strange that a trained lawyer should be readily able to offer a plausible resolution to a legal conflict than that a trained art dealer or tradesman should be readily able to assess a work of art or build houses.

This spontaneous psychological process should not, however, be confused with the final judicial decision which will later appear as a well-argued decision showing full logical accordance among: (1) the major premise: the rule of law selected, (2) the minor premise: the legal fact expressed in terms of the rule, and (3) the conclusion: the logical deduction: judgement and consequences in law. The psychological decision is the motivational process which *leads to* or causes the judicial decision. The judicial decision as later described is the legally controlled deduction which *legitimises* the psychological decision by showing that it is grounded in authoritative and valid rules. While the two processes, the psychological and the logical, may not be confused, there is no reason to separate them. It is our right, and possibly duty, to assume that the two processes are two sides of the same coin and that the account of the legal grounds is identical with the psychological motives which led to the decision. It is true that judicial decisions may be abused to legitimise given interests out of considerations irrelevant to the case. But until the opposite has been proved, we must for reasons of the trust necessary for social cohesion assume that motive and grounds coincide and that the decision maker speaks the truth.

In return, we must request that the legal writer, whether speaking hypothetically or as dogmatist or factually as decision maker, gives an open account of his choices and values both in his selection and interpretation of the legal material as well as in his selection and description of the legal facts. And, indeed, recent legal usage does show an increasing tendency to state openly the considerations which have directed the court in its ranking and analysis of the legal and factual material.

ALF ROSS'S THEORY

Alf Ross's theory of law constitutes a fascinating intellectual and moral *tour de force*. As noted above, any philosophy is determined by a given conscious or subconscious ideology. As for other Scandinavian and American realist theories, Ross's theory was the expression of a certain political ideology, the welfare state's perception of law as a legal instrument. Law is the means of control used by the state for promoting the welfare of its citizens. While American realism based its theory on a sociological model, the Scandinavian realism was by and large copied from a psychological model, albeit behaviourism, which can be said to constitute a psychological theory copied from a sociological model. Taking socio-psychology as its model, Scandinavian realism viewed law as a tool by which to "internalise" certain socially "desirable" attitudes, while to the outside observer, the American attitude aimed at measuring the likelihood of a certain behaviour or response on the basis of certain influences or stimuli.

As noted, American realism was an offshoot of pragmatism, the criterion of truth of which was the achievement of a successful result within the framework of reference adopted. The criterion determining the existence of law was therefore the result of the function of the legal actors, from which it was deduced from an Anglo-Saxon perspective that it must be the judge, as the main actor, who decided what was existing law ("law in action", not "law in books"). And indeed, Oliver Wendell Holmes (1841-1935), who was part of the circle of William James and T. Dewey, the pioneers of psychology and pragmatism, defined law as "prophesies about what the judge will do" in the actual case. On the other hand, the most extreme formulation of the judicial decision is found in Jerome Frank (1889-1957) who views all motives, legal as well as non-legal, as relevant for the interpretation of the content of "law". By placing the main emphasis on the individual decision and on the prediction of the result of the motivational chain, the model for the description of the law becomes "the bad man's law", that is to say the lawyer's perspective in the assessment of the chances of winning a case.

Just as the American realism in terms of political ideology belonged in a liberal instrumental environment culminating in the New Deal politics of the 30s, which was built on state intervention, the Scandinavian realism culminated in the construction of the welfare state in the 30s under social democratic leadership. The issue at stake was the deployment of the rule of law as an educational tool to create a general *sense* of duty. The rule of law was not perceived as the result of an already existing morality, but as the cause for developing moral attitudes.

The same ideology later came to dominate the socialist regimes of Eastern Europe which constitutionalised Hans Kelsen's (1881-1971) purely instrumental concept of law, a concept which identified law and state to the extent where teaching in legal theory had to proceed under the title "Theory of law and state". Kelsen, who had roots in the Viennese circle of logical positivists in the 20s, without further ado defined law as commands supported by the state's monopolised apparatus of force. As noted, the British "Oxford philosophy" or "analytical" philosophy took its basis in the traditional British "common sense" philosophy, consequently viewing the task of legal theory as the analysis of legal language, and from the British as well as the American perspective this meant as a matter of course the language of judges' decisions. H.L.A. Hart and A.M. Honoré's *Causation in the Law* (1959) is the prototype of the theory which analyses or defines "causation" by listing and systematising judicial decisions on the extent of liability. What the courts *actually do or say* expresses what is valid law. To Hart, the "rule of recognition" is a sociological fact which for every judicial system sets the criteria for the production of duties under the law, and in England this is primarily the courts. On the other hand, the law may be compared with game rules which explain the behaviour of the players and therefore becomes a key by which legal behaviour can be understood.

Alf Ross's theory of law as expounded in his work *On Law and Justice* (1953) should be seen against the triple background of Hans Kelsen's theory of state imperatives and sanctions, the socio-psychological theory of "shared ideology" of the Scandinavian realism, and the British analytical theory of game rules as explanatory keys. American realism also plays a role, but rather a negative one in the sense that the behaviouristic model of prognosis is rejected with reference to his own model, which, he argues, has no concrete, but a "general" character, and does not give equal ranking to all factors which motivate the judge. Ross concedes that duties under the law are important, but as his is a realist theory, it is the "sense of duty" which is decisive, and as it is also a general theory, it is interested not in the feelings of the individual judge but rather a "shared ideology of judges". This "shared ideology of judges" contains the rules which make it possible in general to predict the behaviour of judges and thus serve as an explanatory key to legal behaviour. Law is thus a combination of legal behaviour and legal ideology, and as information on the legal ideology cannot be gained except by reading the reasonings contained in judgements, these become the only source of information on valid law. It is therefore of crucial importance that one can trust the judge's reasons, and Ross is doubtful of this, because according to the rule sceptics, the reasoning may be a "surface legitimation" of decisions quite differently motivated.

What is even worse for his theory is the fact that it is based on a concept called "shared ideology of judges", a concept which comes into conflict with his theory of science. It must here be remembered that "law and justice" is not a general theory of law or an analysis of the concept of law such as were Kelsen's pure doctrine of law, "*Reine Rechtslehre*" or Hart's "Concept of Law".

Ross wanted to write a book on jurisprudence and on how to decide in scientific terms what "applies", i.e. what is actually existing Danish law. He adopted the theory of science of logical positivism, which is a theory of language and the conditions of truth of language propositions. As noted above, this theory claimed that "reality" exists and is directly and intuitively transformed into language terms which enabled direct comparisons between the proposition and reality through a method of measuring which made it possible to "verify" or "falsify" the semantic content of the term. A term can be "meaningless" if it lacks "semantic reference", i.e. there is nothing in reality which can be used for comparison. Terms covering "metaphysical" phenomena such as God or angels, or values which do not express attributes of things but the feelings of the person performing the valuation, have no "semantic reference". They are meaningless nonsense, as Ross states.

What Ross is looking for in particular is "justice" as an argument for a position in law. "Justice" is a relic from the old idealist philosophy of law which was not amenable to "scientific" control, because it was a projection on to reality of subjective ideas and values. Therefore, Ross says, terms such as "justice" and "shared Danish sense of law" have no "semantic reference": they are "nonsense arguments", "bangings on the table" like other emotional outbursts. What Ross fails to notice is that by this statement he pulls the carpet out from under his own concept of law, which he identifies as the Danish "shared ideology of judges". It goes without saying that this does not mean the conscious experience by Danish judges of what is Danish law. One need merely consider the existence of disagreements between judges and of reversed verdicts to see with all clarity that any "shared ideology" in that sense is a fiction. At any rate, it will only be able to be "verified" through proper sociological studies and not through the verification apparatus constructed by Ross: the likelihood (above 50%) that a case involving a given rule will be determined in favour of the rule. How is one to decide whether the likelihood is better than 50%? Is it not rather the case that the person making this assessment assesses the legal source material directly, and not the likelihood of the result of the judicial decision? And is this in any case a realistic description of the working method of dogmatics?

Clearly, Ross's theory is untenable. It is undermined by his scientific conditions both because according to his theory, the concept "shared ideology of judges" is "metaphysical", and because according to the same theory, one cannot be sure that the indication of the judge's "sense of duty" given in the premises is true. For according to the theory, the judicial decision is the result of value judgements which cannot be controlled, unless one proceeds on the moral premise that there is agreement between motive and grounds, and this is precisely what Ross does not do.

It is equally clear that there is no basis in the theory for measuring the degree of likelihood of the result of a judicial decision. Finally, and as Illum especially has stressed, it is a "superfluous detour" to attempt to prognosticate the judge's decision. Firstly, it will be difficult to distinguish between prognosis and assessment of legal sources, and secondly there is no particular basis for assuming that judges are better at assessing legal source materials than jurists. On the Continent, judges in general do not rank higher than other jurists. In France the jurists of parliament are "dignitaries" because the parliament is the legal centre, and in Germany and Scandinavia, university jurists traditionally hold a high status. To this should be added that in his dogmatic works, Ross himself followed the traditional direct analysis of legal source materials without applying his own scientific theory.

The theory's greatest weakness is thus a result of the logical positivist scientific theory and its naïve-realist verification apparatus, which may hold some meaning in the natural sciences and in logic, given the strict formal symbolic systems of these sciences. But in disciplines such as the science of law, which deal with phenomena expressed in an adjusted daily language, it is impossible to talk of an "objective" description, which is of course a precondition of the verification system.

We have seen above how the hermeneutic philosophy of language moved the borders of description and evaluation, claiming that all description contains an element of interpretation regarding the concepts' intentional or functional and value-loaded or ideological character. One does not "describe", one "ascribes", that is to say one orders or qualifies phenomena into language concepts on the basis of methods of analogy or comparison.

The borders for the study of law and legal policies do not, therefore, as Ross assumes, run between "description" and "interpretation", statements of advice to the courts, *de sententia ferenda*, but between the latter and statements of advice to the legislature, *de lege ferenda*. The study of law cannot, therefore, be limited to a "description" and "systematisation" of legal rules: interpretation is an essential element in its method.

The study of law is a practical science which must offer advice in legal usage, not just to judges, but also to lawyers in the administration, and other decision makers with legal capacity. The jurist whose theoretical studies reveal systematic flaws or flaws of content in the system of rules also has an obligation to exercise a *critical* function as adviser to the legislature, as it is impossible to provide qualified advice on the changes of laws unless one has an accurate grasp of the existing state.

To advise the courts remains, however, an important function. On the one hand, courts cannot be specialists, but on the other they are constantly confronted with borderline cases which can only with difficulty be "described" or assigned to the existing system. Courts are therefore often faced with the need to fit new experiences or new developments into the existing legal system, and will therefore have difficulty at the start in establishing a dogmatic form, the language of which justifies the decision relative to the law.

In such cases it is the task of the study of law to be "creative" and to find the formula by which the new decisions may be fitted into the system. It is this interplay between theory and practice which characterises the *"Nordic realism"*, the roots of which go back to the work of A.S. Ørsted (1778-1860) in the early 1800s, and which were developed further by A. Aagesen (1826-79), A.C. Evaldsen (1841-1912), C. Goos (1855-1929) and later Julius Lassen (1847-1923), C. Torp (1855-1929) and Viggo Bentzon (1861-1937), and which constitutes another line in the factors influencing Ross's realism.

Similarly to Viggo Bentzon, Ross does not recognise any "normative" legal source theory but claimed a "descriptive" one. It must, on this point also, be the judge's premises from which information was to be gained on what judges recognised as legal source factors, that is to say, arguments and ranking of arguments found acceptable as support for a judicial decision. Clearly, the legal source theory can be countered by the same fundamental objections as the theory of law. To this should be added that there is a need for a platform of criticism of judgements passed. A normative legal source theory of some kind must therefore be adopted, unless one wants to exclude oneself from any criticism of the grounds on which judgements are based.

Thus it cannot be judges alone who, as some "authoritative forum", establish the criteria for the "validity" of the law. As Illum has stressed, all lawyers are part of the profession which, by its shared training and induction into a "legal method", jointly can and must establish the "criteria of truth" applying to assertions on the validity of the law and legal source materials. Neither is it possible, therefore, to reduce the "law" to an empirical phenomenon, behaviour, or feeling (ideology). The concept of law contains a normative element, the concepts of "right" and "duty", the existence of which, as noted, is the precondition for the use of concepts such as "responsibility" and "rights" in *judicial* procedures.

Although the grounds for judgements cannot define what are "valid legal source materials", judges nevertheless remain an important source of information on the existing perception of legal source materials, and a study of the grounds on which judgements are passed can therefore also provide information on how attitudes to the law and social circumstances change with time.

While in the early part of this century the courts applied a formalistic reasoning technique in harmony with the position of high respect in which law and order were held by the "bourgeois democracy", more and more references are found in the years before and after World War II to the motives of the law and to administrative practice, references which were accepted as good arguments. This development is linked with the growth of the "welfare state" and thus with the growth of administrative legislation.

In contrast, recent decades have seen an increasing trend towards recognition of normative values, not only in the form of references to the rule of law, but also towards the use of more direct values such as fairness and equity beside teleological and pragmatic values. References are also found to previous judgements and to the theory of law which were formerly assigned to editorial notes or comments by the High Court.

The analysis of Ross's theory given here must not lead the reader to think that the theory was "poor". Quite the contrary, among outstanding jurists of recent Nordic history, Ross is arguably the one to have insisted most urgently on the necessity of an analysis of the philosophy of law on the basis of current jurisprudence, and to have formulated the legal philosophy of his time on an independent basis. Like all scientists he was circumscribed by the conceptual horizon of his time. He was spokesman for the best qualified theory of science of his time and he transplanted it to the study of law with inveterate consistency and elegance.

Logical positivism was overtaken by developments in science.

Its main fault was its naïve and uncomplicated view of the relationship between language and reality. This simplification was originally dictated by a noble concern to protect science against the abuse of ideologies, and it was therefore an irony of fate that it became the main enemy of a new generation wanting to introduce "critical reason" into science, the absence of values of which exposed it to accusations of being reactionary, that is to say political.

Another weakness was the fact that Ross wanted to transfer the verification procedures of logical positivism which were adapted to the natural sciences on to an area where it was so eminently impossible to reduce language to abstract symbols as in the science of law. The outcome was predictable. Jurists, including Ross himself, continued to use their thousand year-old interpretative methods which were better suited to the more recent hermeneutic philosophy of language and theory of science.

It is the obligation of every generation to clarify its philosophical and scientific foundations. It cannot, therefore, be right that almost 40 years after Ross launched his theory of "existing law", legal scientists continue without reflection to use fragments of this theory such as "semantic reference" and "practicability", and continue to assume without reflection that the courts establish authoritatively what is "valid law", if only for the reason that it is little help to judges themselves to be told to do what they are doing. As is evident from recent reasoning practice, judges are willing to be taught, also by the study of law.

RULES AND PRINCIPLES

The recognition of the hermeneutic character of language excludes any possibility of an "objective" description. Consequently, reality is not "rational", i.e. structured in a logical form of language, and cognition is limited to projections of our reason, or our ideas, but reality exists prior to our knowledge of it.

We must therefore presume that human beings have an "intuitive" ability to translate reality into language concepts directly, or presume that language is an inherited ability, similar, for example, to the ability to walk upright, but which requires development just as our other abilities do. This view is supported by insights from the fields of psychology and neurology. The developmental psychologist J. Piaget has shown that language is more than a learned routine and that consciousness is more than an empty vessel filled through experience. By studying language development in children, Piaget was able to observe that the ability to speak "correctly" developed normally, although children "practise" speaking with other children. From this, Noam Chomsky drew the conclusion that language must contain a "deep structure", which is common to all languages and which explains why human beings are able to form abstract concepts and to encode them in certain structures, thus giving "meaning" to a message which may be passed from person to person.

Grammar and syntax contain the logical rules of language which enable us to form an unlimited number of messages with a limited number of words. This "deep grammar" also makes it possible to "translate" from language to language, although the individual languages or language groups have different "surface structures".

There is, for example, a fundamental difference between "analytical" languages, to which group all Indo-European languages belong, which build on a distinction between subject and object, and "synthetic" languages, which are structured by adding parts to the word stems. It is a plausible theory that this structural peculiarity has contributed to the formation of an "instrumental" consciousness in the European culture, as the language signals in advance that somebody can do something about something. This peculiarity may also explain the development of an analytical written language, "alphabetic writing", in the European area, while Oriental cultures have also developed a synthetic written language, "sign writing". During the Renaissance, western Europe developed partly a technological science and partly a theory on human competence to make laws. Together these two developments can be seen as a result of the perception of the human being called individualism, which says in essence that human beings are the masters of both their physical and social realities.

To lawyers this is a reminder that technology and human rights are mutually connected. The individualistic view of human nature must see the individual as equipped with "rights", that is to say interests which may be claimed through judicial procedures, while a collective view of human nature (symbiosis of subject and object) perceives the whole as the primary unit and the individual as a constituent part, which may therefore be dealt with according to "administrative procedures", under which the interests of the whole are the determining factor (social utility, the idea, the people, the community). If this theory is right, a "logical" connection must be presumed to exist between technology and democracy (the rule of law), such that Japan, for example, will not in the long term be able to develop a high technological social organisation while retaining a collectivist one.

Neurophysiology has demonstrated that language ability is associated with a defined area in the left temple region of the brain, and that any damage to this region has consequences for the ability to think and act rationally. More than 150 years ago Esajas Tegnér pointed to the nature of language and thought as two sides of the same coin when he said that what is obscurely said is obscurely thought. The connection is, however, complicated and much disputed, although no more so than that agreement exists as to the "organic" character of the nature of language, that is to say, its interconnection with other abilities which have the task of maintaining the individual organism and which therefore must be available as a tool for "purposes" set by the organism. Along this road we gain a tentative confirmation of Aristotle's perception of the human being as a social animal or *"zoon politicon"*, as the purpose of human language is the same as for the signal systems of other animals, namely to mediate the communication which is a prerequisite of organised group cooperation.

Recent scientific research has thus supported the philosophical assumption that language is instrumental in character, and as it is linked to our other actions it follows that it must be subject to our unconscious feelings and interests. There is therefore nothing strange in the fact that "light", "warmth", "soft" and "round" are normally positive words, while "dark", "cold", "hard" and "angular" are normally negative words. The values ascribed to the words reflect fundamental human needs or anti-needs. The fact that we embody our interests in the terms we use may also be seen in the manner in which we characterise a revolutionary by either calling him a "freedom fighter" or a "terrorist", or when we choose the term "individualist" or "egotist" to characterise a person who is either an "anarchist" or "asocial", which are the respective Greek and Latin terms for people who place themselves outside society.

In Gulliver's Travels, Jonathan Swift relates how the Lilliputians ransack the pockets of the imprisoned Gulliver and the trouble they had in describing his snuff box, as they were not familiar with the habit. In his thesis, on the perception of the behaviour of others, *Om oplevelsen af andres adfærd* (1953), Franz From shows the impossibility of describing a situation without imparting "meaning" to it, that is to say assuming certain purposes on the part of those involved, as otherwise the description will deteriorate into an endless account of movements in time and space with no connection. If we want to define a "chair" or a "table", we are similarly compelled to include the purpose of the item, as the "table" is for placing something on, while the "chair" is for sitting on, and the "bed" for sleeping in.

The open-ended and thus "generative", that is to say creative, character of language is linked with the peculiarity that concepts can assume different meanings in different contexts. A "house" may thus be a human dwelling, a dog's house, an audience or meeting, a political institution, or a family. Associations tied to the concepts can be transferred to new meanings as part of the process of adding new elements to our experience, which are then assigned to a concept through an analogical process of comparison and by the force of a predominant "similarity". Concepts found in daily language use generally cover "types", in contrast to scientific concepts which are "defined", i.e. accurately delimited in relation to the continuum of the external world, and concepts of type are therefore particularly well-suited for the labelling of those normal cases which constitute the core of our interests, while through a tentative evaluative process of interpretation they can be made to include an indefinite number of phenomena. A well-known example is the concept "forest" which contains no information of how many trees are required or in what grouping or density they should be placed.

It follows naturally from this that language and hence legal language must be structured to suit that part of reality in which we are interested, and that it should take its starting point in those "conditions of life", especially our social needs, which we have established through our culture-generating abilities. As noted, Carl von Savigny (1776-1861) rejected the rationalist system of natural law, preferring to start with the existing, i.e. pre-legal, facts, in German called *Lebensverhältnisse*, and the associated institutions or *Rechtsverhältnisse*. As we saw, the ghost returned and contributed to the formation of a logically systematised "jurisprudence of concepts".

Although we must guard against using irrational concepts such as "institution" as the basis of a general theory of law, we should not suppress the fact that legal control must take its basis in the "pre-legal" facts which people want to use as species and creators of culture. What we must not do is to assume uncritically that "existing" institutions, such as they are, should form the basis of the control. This was precisely the attitude expressed in the Medieval and primitive concept of law as a "reflection" of custom, which is the source of all law. Since the Renaissance, we have recognised the human competence to make laws and the nature of law as a means of social control and change. The more recent so-called "reflexive" theory of law is actually not a theory of law, but part of the sociology of law which is the ideological exponent of a particular view of the relationship between the rule of state and self-governing organs or mechanisms in which greater stress is placed on "grassroots" than on "market economic" mechanisms.

It is clear that a view of language such as here described, implies that law is and must be more than just a system of "norms" and "rules", to be described and interpreted in accordance with some defined language content.

As we have seen, the rules of law are tied to ordinary interests and functions, just like other language terms, but as we have also seen, the rules of law have the special purpose of influencing reality, i.e. human behaviour, in a particular manner or a particular direction, authoritatively. But apart from this, any system of law is also part of a political system and hence of a dominant ideology and an underlying culture and perception of human nature. When we "interpret" legal rules, it must therefore be on the basis of this general system of ideas (ideology) which underpins our systems of language and law.

We have already noticed that the perception of human nature and society of the western world is individualistic, in so far as the individual is seen as society's smallest unit, each of which units may constitute the purpose of society, but not its means. The concept of human rights is a derivation of this view of individual human beings as sovereign citizens, whose personal freedom entitles them to participate in the organisation of society (the social contract, democracy) and in the organisation of their "private" affairs (the principle of contract, private autonomy).

Competing with this principle of freedom is the "principle of equality", which when formulated as the principle of formal equality is aimed at protecting the "rights" of individuals and delimiting the freedom of individual persons as against the equal right of freedom of others (Kant). This formal equality ensures that individuals are treated with equality without regard to rank, estate or ideology — within the framework of the various categories of the law, and that the protection of life and property is safeguarded through the predictability of the law. The object of the judicial procedure is to ensure that these ideals or principles are realised in so far as decisions in conflicts between state and citizen and mutually between citizens are settled by independent and impartial jurors who must follow fixed procedures: openness, contradiction, *audiatur et altera pars*, freedom to consider evidence, direct and oral proceedings and the requirement of authoritative grounds based on valid reasoning from "recognised legal sources", and by application of "recognised legal method".

This whole network of procedural guarantees ensures a "judicial" procedure, which, in contrast to "administrative" procedures, protects the "rights" of individual citizens. When substantive rules of law are applied, it is of course essential that the fundamental values underpinning the constitution and the procedural system are included in the considerations on which the interpretation of the rules is based. The "rule of law" is a fundamental value in constant competition with "social utility" or "reasons of state" which form the foundation of the substantive content of legislation in the modern welfare state.

Constitutional law must be understood and interpreted against the background of the political system and cannot remain untainted by the dominant ideology. As noted, Ross and other legal realists were primarily legal positivists and therefore tended to place a restrictive interpretation on the Constitution where it limited the legislative competence especially in regard to the protection of private property. Ross found no other limits than the impossibility of abolishing the right of private property without a change in the constitution. Currently, and similarly to previous "liberal democratic" or "conservative" periods, the reigning tendency is to draw strict limits for encroachments on "human rights". Considerations of clarity and authority continue to play a role in determining the stand which must be adopted in an interpretation of the constitutional part of the legal system.

Other parts of public law must similarly respect the demand for firmness and consistency, while, as noted, court practice exhibits a stronger element of scepticism in its attitude to efficient administration, in so far as references to administrative practices and the purpose of administration must increasingly give way to considerations of "the administration of law". Abuse of power, i.e. abuse of administrative powers for irrelevant purposes, entails invalidity, and faults in the administrative procedure can have the same consequence. The principle of equality increasingly supplements the principle of legality, such that the administrative procedures approach the judicial also in cases where administrative discretionary powers must be exercised.

Bankruptcy law is based on the principle of equality such that any interpretation of the rules of privileges in case of bankruptcy must take its starting point in the fact that such privileges require special authority. Related to this is the rule prohibiting the use of analogy in criminal law, which is an expression of the general principle of individualism, which in turn forms the basis of our political ideology. Nobody can be punished without explicit authority in law, *nulla poena sine lege*, and nobody is guilty until the prosecution has proved guilt.

Private law is also an expression of this fundamental individualism, which takes its basis in the right of private property which may only be subject to discretionary restriction against compensation, and a contractual freedom based in the principle of private autonomy. More recently, recognition of the principle of material equality has led to an increasing number of restrictions on private freedom and, in step with the construction of a large public sector, the level of taxation has been raised and the means obtained for controlling the private sector.

Nevertheless, the intention of the parties remains the basis of any interpretation of the promise given by the parties, although it is not necessarily decisive for the determination of the extent of the rights and duties of the parties. Here objective legal considerations must often supplement the unpredictable consequences of the agreement — breach, for example — which consequences are often specified in supplementary legal provisions or legally binding private provisions in the form of standard conditions (agreed documents, authorised conditions and partly one-sided conditions). Where the making of law involves persons in a strategic position of fundamental equality, it must generally be more open-ended in order to allow for a greater degree of analogous conclusions, for example, based on the assumption that contract law such as the Danish Contract Act, Sale of Goods Act etc. are embodiments of general legal principles which may be applied also to areas not regulated by law. The Motives to the Contract Act state explicitly that the rules governing invalidity are not exhaustive, and the Sale of Goods Act can be applied quite extensively to the purchase of real estate, although both assumptions are less certain now than before.

In comparison, the provisions of the Property Act, which govern relations with external people, are as a rule indispensable, as the parties might otherwise be allowed an opening for private "abuse of power", through which they may cause harm to a third party. Social considerations may of course also limit the scope for analogy and transactions by the parties in so far as it is in the interest of society to protect the parties against selling their birthright for a dish of lentils.

We have seen how "material justice" has also been rehabilitated in the present time, where there is no need to consider oneself excluded by reasons of "logic" from using that kind of fundamental value judgement. "Equity" and "reasonableness" are expressions which are gaining an increasing hold in legislation (Danish Contract Act, Section 36) and in the reasoning of judges, even outside statutory cases. One must of course handle such uncontrollable concepts with care, but one should not, on the other hand, suppress such value judgements or hide them under the cover of objective expressions, such as "practicality", "factual reasons", "likely" or other such rhetorical tricks which cover personal value judgements. Value judgements should be analysed and verbalised as far as possible and further subjected to a typological division in accordance with the usual dogmatic legal method.

There is thus no reason to distinguish between "rules" and "principles" as two different categories of norms, as some more recent theories of law would have it. This distinction is based on the naïve perception of language prevalent among the analytic and realist theories, a perception which was based on the idea of the objective nature of language and therefore on the ability to make an objective description of rules and facts. The consequence of this misunderstanding was that it had to be assumed that there were "holes" in the system of rules, which judges had to close with more or less *ad hoc* decisions. The purpose of the theories which made principles a separate source of law was to close the system of rules in order to make it exhaustive, so that there would always be one and only one "right" solution to a conflict in law.

Quite apart from their lack of proper language analysis, it is unsatisfactory that such theories should attempt to deny the existence and necessity of value judgements in the application of law and the study of law. An adequate language analysis would in fact find that the interpretation and application of law always involves an element of value judgement, in so far as a "description" in language terms will always constitute an interpretation made on the background of a particular situation in life, including the external worlds of politics, ideology and culture underpinning the legal system.

MODEL AND ANALOGY

As noted above, new experiences cannot become conscious knowledge without having undergone an analogical, or comparative, mental process by which they are assigned to one of the already incorporated concepts or conceptual systems.

The word "concept" also expresses the idea that parts of reality are "grasped" and held by the conscious mind in a fixed form in a way which allows this conscious content to be fetched from memory and brought into use in later similar situations, like other "tools". Psychology teaches that the difference between an "aid" and a "tool" is precisely this "conscious content", which makes it possible to store a suitable aid for future use, so that the person does not have to seek and form his or her aids every time.

Any such transfer from "aid" to "tool" presupposes a *sense of identity*, i.e. the person's consciousness of being the same person from one moment to another and from one place to another. For the sense of identity to become a concept of identity and the sense of time to become a concept of time, the sense of identity is thus also conditional upon a sense of time. Consequently, *the use of tools* is considered by modern psychology to be the decisive criterion for the concept of man, as several animal species, not least our close relatives the chimpanzees, have the ability to use aids in order to satisfy their needs, but not to use "tools".

Our concept formation is thus functional, and must therefore always be dependent on existing needs. These needs change with any change in culture resulting from the ability of human beings to change their surroundings by using their picture-generating consciousness. While animals live according to their instinctive behaviour, which ensures the survival of the species, people, who are very poor in instincts because of the freedom which their consciousness has given them to adapt their surroundings to their purposes, must develop new forms of consciousness, rules as surrogates for lost instincts.

Depending on the speed of cultural "development", people will surround the organisational rules of their society with different associations. If development is relatively slow, the model or analogy preferred will be associated with *custom*, which is seen as an expression of an eternal or natural moral code or law, generally of divine origin. Primitive societies of the past made no distinction between morality and law. The Greek word "ethics" and the Latin word "morality" both derive from the word for "custom". When social change happens more quickly, the perception of law also changes. It is separated from morality in step with the emergence of the view that human beings have the supreme right to change society without the help of God, and as a consequence of an instrumental view of man, the concept of law comes to mean: *means of control*. Law is associated with either an act of will (command), or a covenant (social contract).

In addition to its status-indicating and controlling functions, the law has traditionally had a conflict-resolving function. The perception of law arising out of this function is the view that the law is either the procedure or the result of the procedure adopted for the purpose of conflict resolution in the society in question.

The characteristic feature of primitive social and legal thinking is that law is *collective, objective and casuistic*. Hunter-gatherer cultures are tied to small collective units which distribute total yields according to fixed distribution norms aimed at maintaining status rankings, but also at protecting those who do not take part in the gathering, but perform other tasks in relation to children and old people. The children represent future provisions, the old have a high status because they represent accumulated experience of great value in static societies. These status- and value-based distribution rules ensure internal peace and external protection for the group's members. Relations with other groups are determined by collaboration or competition and are subject to collective sanctions, as no other option for *enforcement of the law* exists than collective reaction, either in the form of threats or retribution which may in principle fall upon any member of the group without consideration being given to individual guilt.

The Mosaic law of the Old Testament represents the transition from a primitive culture to a higher nomadic or agrarian culture, where territorial interests create a need for a new concept to cover "property rights", which are of little significance in a society with no permanent settlements and where houses and tools are of less permanent value. Family and inheritance law therefore gain increasing importance with greater permanence of settlements and accumulation of values in land and stock. The Indo-European word for "property" is derived from the same word as "lineage".

According to the Old Testament the law was given by Jehovah, in Moses' encounter with him on Mount Sinai, from where Moses brought back the law hewn in stone tablets. In contrast to other Mediterranean cultures, e.g. Egyptian and Mesopotamian law, the law was not given to the people but agreed in a covenant, which is binding on both God and the people. The family is now the foundation of society. Responsibility is collective with inheritance to the seventh issue, and it is objective as the unlimited right of retribution is restricted to *talion*, that is *equal* retribution and in many cases replaced by fines.

The *contractual element* as built into Jewish thought was, however, to exert a major influence on the thinking of later times, when the Mediterranean cultures developed an *urbanised* culture tied to the ever-increasing division of labour which followed on the heels of developments in trade, commerce and navigation. Against this background, a new view of society and the law was emerging in Jewish urban societies based on an *individualistic* perception of human nature, according to which human value is not measured by customary status, but by the results of the individual effort. Children, the old and the weak lose their value, so a new ethic must be developed based on charity and individual responsibility. This new ideology developed gradually in the years following the Babylonian captivity around 450 BC and culminated in the radical moral injunctions of the Christianity of the New Testament.

At the same time, a similar change took place in the other Mediterranean cultures. Homer's heroic poems reflect historical events around 1000 BC (the time of Moses), but are the result of an oral tradition transfixed in one or more written versions with the introduction of writing in Greece in the middle of the first millennium before our time. At any event, in the 7th century BC, Draco's laws were written down on columns of stone at the *agora* of Athens, and they represent the transition between an objective and a subjective view of man by ascribing significance to negligence in the reaction to manslaughter and by developing cities or places of *asylum* as the Old Testament had done. Asylum derives from the Greek word *sylon*, which means robbery, or robbery of temples; *asylon* means sanctuary for robbery. The purpose was to dampen aggressive and retributive actions for a period until a commutation into fines could be negotiated.

At the time of Solon (6th century BC), Athens' constitution and legal system were revised, and the debts of the old landed gentry to the merchants of the city were commuted, and distraint on the person abolished. The spreading of a money economy had led to a growth in inflation which had undermined the fortunes of land owners because of a shortage of labour on the land. Money had become the yardstick by which social value was measured in contrast to status and honour in the surviving aristocratic society.

Aristotle later told how Solon extended the traditional concept of justice based on equality of services (commutative) to include distributive justice, meaning that *organised* society possessed the resources required to redistribute values created by the community on the basis of an evaluation of the importance of individual persons for society (social utility). This social evaluation is different from that of primitive *organic* societies which is based on *status relations* rather than on *contractual relations* as is the case in organised societies. Aristotle provides an account of the connection between contractual relations and democracy, i.e. the representative government at the time of Solon and later, the model of which is to be found in the *social contract*. The Sophists who developed a rationalist and analytic philosophy and argumentation technique in the 400s rejected the idea of the gods as the creators of man. They believed instead that man had created the gods in their image and with the aid of reason had created the organisation and laws of society in the same manner. This individualistic and instrumental view of law led to an absolute democratic social control which left it to the *public assembly* not only to pass laws but also to resolve conflicts in law.

It was Aristotle's view that this view of the law led to cynicism and selfishness, and after the defeat in the Peloponnesian War around 400 BC, Plato, and after him Aristotle, argued for an *ethical* restriction in the competence to make laws. Plato wanted to achieve this through enlightened despotism, while Aristotle instead demanded a restriction of democracy through a restriction of the freedom tied to ordinary laws so that these could no longer be changed arbitrarily by the popular assembly. For Aristotle assumed human beings to be not only reasonable beings but also social beings (*zoon politicon*), with a special *natural* inclination towards rational order. This classical theory of natural law was to gain great importance in later ages.

While the Greeks were thus in the process of developing not only politics, but ethics and rhetoric as well, they did not create special procedures for private conflict resolution and thus a legal profession. That was left to the Romans. There are admittedly elements in the *Iliad* which indicate that conflicts between families were settled through special arbitrators, and there is a shield showing Dice throwing her staff between Achilles and Hector and thus interceding between the parties in an attempt to arbitrate. But it was the Romans who developed the professional (private) arbitration institutes requiring professional legal advisers for the submission of opinions. On the basis of these opinions, a system of legal interpretation and supplementation of the law of the Twelve Tables was established, which according to legend had been published after the Greek model at the *Forum Romanum* c. 450 BC Like the Greek dramas from the middle of the 400s, as seen in the transition from Aeschylus' *Oresteia* to Sophocles' *Antigone*, these original laws span the movement from a collective and objective family responsibility to an individual and subjective responsibility with a basis in natural law.

In the 5th century BC a shared Mediterranean culture thus developed, based on an individualistic and instrumental view of man and law. While the Greek model is political and constructed from an analogy to the concept of the covenant, the social contract, the Roman model, is process-oriented and tied to a professional interpretation and argumentation technique borrowed from Greek philosophy. Based on this dual influence of Stoic and Christian ideology, the Roman model of the process system grew during the classical and post-classical period into a well-developed legal conceptual arsenal culminating in the Justinian codification (AD 529) after the collapse of the West Roman Empire (AD 476).

Under the influence of the less developed cultures of the Germanic peoples, the law and the concept of law deteriorated. Roman law became vulgarised as the agrarian economies and feudal social structures had no need for or understanding of the old more highly urbanised culture's more refined rules and concepts. No commercial law is needed, for example, where no commerce takes place! *Corpus Iuris* sank into oblivion, but was presumably still to be found in the cities of northern Italy, where trade and navigation again gathered strength in the centuries up to AD 1000. At all events, a special Lombardian law of commerce developed which gradually served to deepen the understanding of a special legal technique.

In due course, a law course proper based on the study of *Corpus Iuris* was introduced at the University of Bologna c. AD 1100. The model of this study was the *scholastic* method which had been developed through the Church schools' rhetorical-dialectic teachings of the *Trivium*, which continued throughout the Medieval period. The Church was the only unifying organised cultural element to survive the fall of the Roman Empire, and the Church attempted to exploit this position in order to succeed to the authority of the Roman Empire both in spiritual as well as secular affairs, including legal matters. The Church represented especially the art of writing which could be utilised to make "authentic interpretations" by writing down the customary law as was done with the Nordic provincial laws. But the Church also laid claim to the Roman Emperor's direct competence as lawmaker, which, it was claimed, had been transferred to the Pope in Rome when Constantine moved the imperial residence to Constantinople.

The early Church fathers' view of human nature and law did, however, reflect the harsh realities which followed upon the collapse. St. Augustine (354-430) expressed this in his *De Civitate Dei*, the City of God, where he stressed the sinfulness of human nature and the need for chastisement by the law of God, which is based on charity, mercy and the protection of the weak. Pope Gelasius (492-496) developed the doctrine of the two swords: the ecclesiastic sword which allowed the Church to establish and enforce the law, and the secular sword which was left to the emperor, who had been granted his authority from God in order that he might defend the helpless, including the people of the Church, and enforce the secular customary law.

The legal model of the Medieval period had fallen back on the idea of a divine customary law, which was not established, but found, by the secular princes. At the height of the Medieval period (1100-1200), the Europeans rediscovered Aristotle's rational philosophy, and with that his theory of natural law through their contact with the Arabs in Spain. The new universities united the scholastic science and the canonic theory of law or Church law with Aristotle's philosophy in their study of the Justinian law book. Thomas Aquinas (1225-75) fused Aristotle's rationalism with the teachings of the Church in his supposition that God's law is the primary law, but that it had only been given in the form of principles which may be specified by the secular authorities in positive law. Although positive law may not conflict with natural law, it must nevertheless be obeyed, unless it also conflicts with the law of God. In contrast to St. Augustine, St. Thomas Aquinas also assumed that human beings have a social nature which makes Church and secular chastisement less urgent.

Subsequent centuries saw the development partly of an ecclesiastic moral philosophy and partly of a secular science of law based on Roman law. Common to both schools of thought was their point of departure in the ideal of science derived from Aristotle and linked with his *teleological* metaphysics. The essential task was to discover the essence of things and thus the purpose of their movement. The natural science ideal thus became authoritative and dialectic, with the result that the earliest science of law assumed a similar dialectic and dogmatic method. The early glossators strove through annotations (glossaries) to establish consistency and coherence in the *Corpus Iuris*, using for the process, as noted, the traditional technique of the *Trivium*. They attempted to explain away discrepancies and fill in vacuums through systematic considerations. This purely theoretical dogmatism dominated science from Irnerius (c. 1100) to Glossa Ordinaria (c. 1250) and was based in the *sic et non* or *pro et contra* of dialectics.

The post-glossators or commentators (c. 1300-1400) had a different objective for their science, so they used partially different methods. The growth in urbanisation during the Renaissance saw a corresponding increase in the division of labour and the money economy, and Europe was again launched on a social development requiring new organisational structures. An individualistic and instrumental perception of human nature gave a spur to the physical and social sciences in step with the awareness that people had the power to change their physical and social surroundings.

William of Ockham rejected Aristotle's teleological metaphysics, arguing that concepts are not attributes of things but names we give to things (nominalism). This doctrine released the natural sciences from speculating on the "essence" of things and enabled it to set out on the development of a functional and mechanistic science of nature. Based on the original view of the people's assembly as the supreme sovereignty, Marsilius of Padua held that the lawmaker's competence properly belonged to the people, a view which culminated in the principle of sovereignty of J. Bodin (1530-96). As a corollary, law schools were now given the task of educating practical lawyers, capable of acting as technical advisers or *commentators* to secular authorities. Consequently, the legal method came to revolve more around an interpretation of Roman law in light of the modern, i.e. feudal, social reality. This included, for example, a transformation of the Roman concept of property rights to cover both a "superior" property right and an "inferior" property right, *dominium directum* and *dominium utile*.

While the two glossary schools relied mainly on dialectic or mathematical methods, *mos italicus*, the "humanist" science of law based in France employed mechanical and physical analogies, *mos gallicus*, to a greater extent. When, in the late 1500s and early 1600s, Copernicus and Kepler had revolutionised the cosmic world map and demonstrated the physical laws governing astronomy, the science of law had also become influenced by the concept of causation. Thus the rationalist natural law theory, founded by Hugo Grotius (1583-1645), stipulated that natural law is eternal and immutable, but that laws also have causes or motives, which are not identical to their grounds. These causes are expressions of the rational principles underlying the law, which are due to human reason. Human reason is therefore capable of directly grasping the rational principles which permeate (the right) legal system.

With roots among the well-to-do Dutch burghers, and holding a positive view of human nature, Grotius had adopted the Aristotelian-Thomist doctrine of man's social nature, and hence the social contract as his model of the law. In contrast, his contemporary Thomas Hobbes (1588-1679) took a pessimistic view of human nature and, based on this, developed a doctrine of natural law which legitimised princely despotism, arguing that in the natural state, people were asocial and selfish creatures requiring a strong government to force them into submission. In Hobbes' version, the social contract is not merely a fiction, but also an empty fiction as its one purpose is to transfer full sovereignty to the prince for the common good. It was this philosophy which served to legitimise among other despotic governments the rule of despotism introduced in Denmark by the Constitution of 1660.

These two models of the social contract reflect the interests of the growing middle classes, and in various mixes led partly to a political development of human rights and democracy as a form of government (J. Locke (1632-1704), J.-J. Rousseau (1712-78)) culminating in the French Revolution of 1789, and partly to the continued development of a legal science based on Roman and natural law, a development which not only refined processes of legal concept formation, but also established a related logical systematics capable of classifying logical deductions and serving as model for codifications of law (S. Pufendorf (1632-94), C. Thomasius (1655-1728), C. Wolff (1679-1754)).

During the 19th century, the situation changed radically. The model of general science became *development* as manifested in biology and electricity. The arts also adopted a biological *organic theory*, and the centre of gravity of the science of law shifted to Germany, where Carl von Savigny, as we have seen, rejected codification, referring partly to matters of a practical nature and partly to ideology.

The practical issues were partly the absence of a unified German nation, partly the lack of scientific analysis of German law. The ideological issues were linked to the conflict between the French radicalism which had established the *Code Napoleon* on the one hand, and the conservative "reaction" dominant among the victors after 1814 on the other. The historical method stressed partly the perspective of development in the law and its interplay with general cultural development and partly its "national" aspect. It is our community by birth, *natio*, with a culture and a people, which forms the basis of social life. The authority on which the law is based is therefore this "spirit of the people" which has been the bed on which both language and law have developed throughout history. Savigny's search takes him back to the traditional "conditions of living" or "institutions" which occasioned the "conditions of law" arising from the *reports nécessaires*, which according to Charles Montesquieu (1689-1755) occupied a position between things and rules, *nature de chose*.

It was this Romantic-idealist theory which dictated both Savigny's and A.S. Ørsted's doctrine of "the nature of things", *Natur der Sache*, which according to both is the proper authority of law. While, ironically, Savigny found the spirit of the German people clearly expressed in the Roman sources of law, Ørsted found it very sensibly in practical needs which he found were expressed in the practice of the law.

Behind this shift of the science of law not only from France to Germany but also from rationalism to idealism lay, however, an undercurrent of social development which was already making itself felt just below the surface in all countries. The industrial revolution in the late 1700s had been mainly a French and British phenomenon, while Germany remained a divided and backward society of farmers and burghers.

While the contract model is a suitable analogy for a society of burghers ideally consisting of enlightened and rational people in the same strategic position, it is clear that a capitalist society requires partly large capital investments, raw materials and markets for the sale of its mass products, and partly greater control and regulation of society. Capital investments require a credit system, especially a well-functioning mortgage credit system, and the servicing of such loans requires long-term planning and firm expectations regarding sales and thus of the profit yield from investments. It is the obligation of the nation state to ensure this task, and it becomes the task of the science of law to sift the legal concepts, rules and systems such that the law becomes a handy tool for facilitating this technical and economic process.

The first task is the separation of law and morality, which is done through the acceptance of Kant's formal concept of morality which leaves the formulation of positive law fully up to the state. On the other hand, the state must keep its hands off private law, which must have liberty to develop freely in light of the "spirit of the people", which is the conservative political-ideological message of Savigny's historical perspective on law. There is therefore nothing strange in the fact that Savigny and his followers gradually developed a "jurisprudence of concepts" which honed the legal concepts and the legal system, allowing the textbooks to be used as models for the codification process set in motion from mid-century when Germany had grown into Europe's strongest military and political power.

From then on, the state enters with greater and greater force into the protection of the weak through protective labour and social laws, after it has appeared that capitalism has radically changed the burghers' strategic position. The social contract is no longer a suitable social and legal model, for it is evident that society is not organised as a rational debate among enlightened people, but as a struggle between interests. In this situation, the law becomes the battleground of conflicting interests (Jhering, Goos).

The interest theory of law led to various "sociological" concepts of *Freirecht* around the turn of the century, which turn the attention back on the judge as the resolver of conflicts, as had been traditionally the case in the Anglo-Saxon perception of law.

During the course of this century we have, as discussed earlier, seen examples of all three types of legal theories which hypostatise one of the various functions: control, codification and conflict resolution. Up to recent decades, the common element of the realist and analytical theories has been their functional control model. The most extreme form has been the theories of command and sanction developed on the basis of logical positivism and Scandinavian realism. Like the democratic socialist theories, these theories have an authoritarian stamp which places the interests of the state and social utility above the security of the life and property of the individual citizen. The analytical theories show less authoritarianism in their rules, which place emphasis on formal justice, but they are instrumental, as is the pragmatic American realism, although less evidently so, because its instrumentalism is concealed in a theory of language which leaves it to the judge to translate reality into language and legal concepts by strength of an intuitive process which escapes control. The analytical theories stand apart precisely because they take no interest in the problem of the judicial decision or legal dogmatism.

Current procedure-oriented theories (Ronald Dworkin), "reflexive" theories (Gunther Teubner) and "discursive" theories (Jürgen Habermas, Niklas Luhmann), "institutional" (O. Weinberger, N. MacCormick) seek new analogies or models in order to legitimise their theories. As mentioned, these new "models" must, like all other models, be seen as hypostases for one of the functions of the law, and as such as a theory based in ideology with no claim to universality. Like earlier models they contain elements of the function of myth as justification of a given ideology or perception of human nature. Nazi and Marxist theories which openly refer to "ideological" issues such as "community of people" or " the people" are in a way less dangerous.

The best way in which to view law is in my opinion partly to hold fast to a *"pluralistic"* perspective which stresses the ability of the law to be perceived in different ways depending on the questions we ask by power of the context which "the law" enters into as a concept, and partly that it is essential to avoid the irrationality consequent upon the intuitive perception of language which either makes an artificial distinction between knowledge and value judgements or leaves all knowledge to intuitive "descriptions".

PLURALIS JURIS

As we have seen, most theories of law and the science of law derive from an emphasis placed on one of the traditional functions of the law, codification, conflict resolution, or control. The former two types are common in less developed societies and in societies which remain dominated by private legal thinking, while the control model coincides with state interference in the private economy.

The perception of law in pre-state societies is tied to the concept of an old sacred custom as the model of the authority of the law. An example from Denmark is the Law of King Valdemar. In a bourgeois liberal society, the perception of law uses the contract, the social contract, as its model, or court decisions, as was the case on the Continent and in Britain respectively. It was not until the conditions for formation of the modern welfare state existed that the administrative control model became a reality. The law does, however, also fulfil other functions than the fixing of rules of competence and procedure, the resolution of conflict or control of social processes.

Indeed the main task of the law is rather to prevent than to resolve conflicts. When attention is directed to "sick" or "hard" cases, a distorted view of the law may result. On the other hand, it is in marginal situations that the law must prove its worth, as there is no need for obligations as long as the parties have an interest in fulfilling each other's expectations. Rules of law are on trial when situations develop differently from what was expected, for example when the parties lose interest in fulfilling a contract or want to leave a marriage. Rules of procedure should not primarily be aimed at protecting the good or those in high esteem, but rather those who do not command the sympathy of their surroundings.

Nonetheless, an important function of rules of law is to limit conflict, and it has significant social value in avoiding human and financial costs arising from the political and legal organisation. As noted, models of law derived from legal sociology or political science are common in current theories of law. Systems theories and cybernetic models have placed emphasis on suppression of the risk of conflict in the complicated modern society through "feedback" and adaptation to other social systems. The problem with these systems theories is that, like the existentialist theories, they view the rules of law merely as a proposal for resolving a potential conflict and not as a normative obligation.

The same applies to the so-called "discursive" theories, which take their ideological stand in the ideal democratic principle: a "rational debate among informed persons" (Habermas) and "reflexive" theories of law (Teubner), which reflect a political attitude in favour of "grassroots procedures" or "autonomy". Theories derived from legal political science, which generally perceives law as an important institution in the modern state formation, discuss to what extent it is possible to maintain simultaneously a state "governed by law" and a "welfare state". Here, "autonomy" is one method, while "privatisation" is another method. In the former case, inspiration may be obtained from the model of "reflexive" law, while in the latter case inspiration may be obtained from a "contract model". This does not, however, change the fact that the models drawn from political science are ideological rewritings of the political ideology adopted as a basis of a criticism of the modern degeneration of the "welfare state" into a "corporate state" or a "people's democracy".

The common element between the "corporate" state of the West and the former people's democracies in the East has been the belief that a superordinary "totalitarian" social ideology would be able to solve all tasks: to create values, to distribute values and to finance social tasks. The incorporation of normative or moral criteria instead of quality has greatly impaired efficiency and strengthened bureaucracy.

Views of the law derived from sociology, political science or the politics of law are important but not focal "perspectives of the law", as in these contexts, the law is perceived as a "social function" on a par with other social functions. When attention is turned to the strictly "legal" function, the normative element, obligation, becomes a central factor in law. To the lawyer, the chance of winning a particular case is of course an important consideration when advising a client, but to the judge it is, as we have seen, irrelevant to be told that "the law" is identical with the decision he is likely to give. And to the study of law that kind of prognosis is equally irrelevant.

The central issue for the legal conflict resolver and the study of law is to find arguments which constitute valid grounds in actual and hypothetical conflicts in law in terms of a specification of the legal norms and a qualification of the "facts of law" within a typology corresponding to the content of the norms.

In this context, the basis must be the "language content", as in a liberal democratic society, *the rule of law* must form the basis of any interpretation of the legal material. "Common language use" is the accepted term for the meaning which the parties are "authorised" to apply (laws must be published). Semantic, syntactic or systematic elements are of course part of this text analysis. Legal usage is of major importance in the illustration of this typology, given that the structure of the law as a rule stresses the *formal* "justice" which dictates that "like cases be treated alike".

In private law, the principles of "intention" and of "expectation" compete for power in the fixing of the declaratory law rules, which "serve the interest of the parties in average terms" but which must be considered in the light of concern for the "safeguarding of turnover" and other interests, the purpose of which is to protect private turnover and security. But in the administrative legislation which regulates and controls private matters of law, the motives of the lawmakers, i.e. the historical preliminary work, enter as an important factor in the establishment of the relationship of purpose and means consequent upon the teleological and pragmatic weighing of "factual considerations" in the case of an alternative interpretation.

In the further argumentation, courts now consider themselves entitled to apply a string of normative (reasonable, equitable) and "rhetorical" (comparative, contrasting) arguments and priorities (*lex superior* vs. *lex inferior*, special vs. general law, recent vs. older law) without it being possible to give fixed rules for the ranking. But as noted, it is necessary to take one's starting point in the *general principles* of the political/cultural system, just as it is necessary to use the *special principles* in special areas of law as a starting point.

This general principle of interpretation follows from what we have said about the general hermeneutic nature of language. Although any description couched in language implies an interpretation, and although the language interpretation of a rule must be seen in relation to certain types of factual situations, this language qualification is neither an "intuitive" process capable of transformation into "general language use" nor "equity", nor an "open-ended" law system allowing a subjective value judgement in the difficult cases.

As in all language use it is both possible and necessary to seek guidance in a systematic interconnection with the values of the ruling cultural system, including the political and parliamentarian system, but also with the fundamental values of the various sub-systems. In the last resort, one must seek an *intersubjective consensus* with the legal profession in general and dogmatic jurisprudence in particular. This intersubjective expert consensus is at all times the only criterion of what is good science.

The principle of rationality must compete with the principle of reality. The rationality principle may lead astray, as has happened in the "jurisprudence of concepts", in the "common-sense" theory and in the study of law in general, because the speculative metaphysics of antiquity has been adopted without reflection, a metaphysics which assumed that in all further transformations, things must follow the same principles as in their constitution.

On the other hand, realism must guard against developing into an anti-theoretical "pragmatism", losing contact with reason and rational control and developing into a "realism devoid of principles".

And the theory of law must abandon all thought of following the "concept of law" into a monistic theory, and instead accept the modern recognition based in relativity theory and liberalism, that any case has several sides to it, and the truth many faces. All concepts can appear in a range of contexts. They must change meaning according to the pertinent questions of the various contexts, and must be answered by the methods relevant to each context.

JUDICIAL DISCRETION

It is clear that the "interpretation" of concepts or qualification of facts as "duress" in Section 29 of the Danish Contract Act, "fraud" in Section 30, "clearly unreasonably" in Section 31, and "common probity" in Section 3, not to mention "unreasonable" terms of Section 36, do not constitute a language interpretation in the same manner as that required for the term "a different content from that intended" of Section 32. As we have seen, the qualification in language of any factual situation involves value judgements, but the expressions quoted involve a different type of evaluation. This is a moral evaluation, but not of an independent personal or even "common" kind. Rather it is a "legal" evaluation involving the mutual balancing of a number of legal considerations: the concern for law and order on the one hand, and on the other the concern for contractual freedom, faith in the general freedom to enter into contracts, and the "safeguarding of turnover"; on top of this, it involves concerns for differences in the parties' strategic positions with regard to level of information, power, dependency, and influence on the formulation of the terms of the contract plus other special circumstances.

Based on the mutual balancing of these various concerns, legal usage has decided which of the parties must carry the risk of the various situations, a usage on which the interpretation which should guide developments of the equity clause of Section 36 has also been based. Only through such typological legal evaluations is it possible to prevent "general clauses" from leading to unpredictability and uncertainty in the law, and this must be the foundation of any use of the law. But interpretations do of course change in step with the general view of the importance of the various interests.

In the same way, "significant breach" as a condition of termination of a contract constitutes a value judgement, which must be based on similar considerations of a legal generalising nature, in order to prevent one of the parties from exploiting a breach of contract to gain release from a contract which he may want to back out of for other reasons. In general, the rules of breach are an inheritance from the Catholic medieval moral philosophy and the rationalist natural law theory of the 1700s and its dogma of "just payment", which ensures the reciprocity, *synallagma*, which has been proposed since antiquity through Aristotle as the primary substantive content of justice.

In labour law the concept of "objective reasons" is applied to the cancellation of an employment contract. It is a widely disputed "political" question of whether, for example, resignation from a given labour union constitutes such an objective reason in cases where no exclusive agreement exists, or in cases of a civil service appointment. This evaluation is influenced by a string of different considerations as to the organisational interests of labour unions on the one hand and considerations of personal liberty on the other, considerations which may be weighted differently from time to time, but which must enter into a general legal evaluation.

From administrative law, we know the concept of "principle of equality". This principle requires that the administrative decision must be based on "objective" criteria, but here too the terms "equality" and "objective" must be understood on the basis of a similar general evaluation of the various criteria for "equality" and "objectivity" in the context of administrative purposes. The administrative discretionary decision is not an independent discretionary decision, but one based in law.

The law of torts and criminal law apply concepts such as "negligence" and "gross negligence" as a condition of assigning responsibility to a person. The concepts do not hold the same content within the two areas, as it may well be relevant to impose liability for damages while acquitting from criminal liability in the same case. When "negligence" is qualified as "gross negligence" it is clear that a more reprehensible behaviour is involved, but it is only through legal evaluation and usage that these concepts are substantiated. Gross negligence is often a refuge of courts wanting to strike at a likely intent.

The fixing of a sentence within the law's maximum and minimum limits is an entirely different evaluation, which cannot in the name of justice be performed independently and arbitrarily, but is gradually fleshed out as a fixed typology through legal usage. In the same manner, the concept of damages and compensation calculations depends on fixed limitations, as only certain types of damages are compensated, and only certain items enter into the calculation of damages. When material damage is involved, the basic principle applied is replacement costs or repair costs, while the sales value is only rarely considered. No compensation is given for sentimental value, and only in certain cases for operating loss. When personal injury is involved, an evaluation of "fairness" is performed involving expenses incurred; loss of income is also compensated, but future and "non-financial" losses only in accordance with certain rates.

The clause covering cause and adequacy is used for legitimation of this risk evaluation, which in practice has developed a certain degree of typology. "Foreseeability" or "predictability" or similar expressions are often applied to justify the limitations relative to the principles which underlie the law of torts as a legal institution, but as noted above, this is pure fiction with no psychological content, as "foreseeability" can have different meanings for different types of damage or injury. When personal injury is involved, one may "predict" heavier consequences than for material damage in most countries.

Even where such a fundamental principle in procedural law as the "freedom to consider evidence" is concerned, it is clear that demands on the quality of evidence differ in different types of cases. In criminal cases a high measure of likelihood of the guilt of the accused is normally required, while in cases under private law and the law of torts, demands may be eased a little both with regard to *culpa* and cause-effect, in order to make it easier for the party to gain compensation. Rules regarding the burden of proof and the weight of evidence vary with the considerations of material law in the various contexts. Thus the burden of proof regarding the extent of an obligation normally falls upon the party making the claim, which accords with the general subsidiary rule of interpretation, which limits the obligation of the debtor (the minimum rule). The burden of proof with regard to cause is eased in cases of tort if the tortfeasor has committed gross negligence, if anonymous defects exist, or if personal injury has occurred, especially where any such fact is competing against unknown causes. Occasionally, the burden of proof is reversed both in contract law and the law of torts in order to increase the material severity of the liability.

Everywhere in the legal system, we find this type of concept operating, concepts which appear to be objective but which contain a value judgement which is essential for the application of abstract rules to factual events, the common "principle of equity". This principle goes back to the oldest science of language as developed by the Sophists in Athens. It was stressed by Plato and adopted by the Romans in the sense of *"aequitas"*, by continental and British medieval law, "equity", and the rationalist natural law theory. These value judgements are not, however, either individual or "intuitive" (common sense), but the result of an application of principles based in practice on the careful weighing of the conflicting legal considerations occurring in various situations of life. The task of the study of law is to assist legal authorities in finding and analysing these concerns, to place them in a systematic context so that they are brought into mutual harmony, and finally to summarise them in legal concepts, maxims and rules of interpretation and legal usage.

NATURAL LAW AND JUSTICE

The idea of justice is closely tied to the idea of a natural law. The idea of natural law has no significance for either the *formal* validity of the law, i.e. the grounding of the law, or for its *substantive* validity, i.e. the moral content of the law (right of reaction), or for the *problem of substantiation*, i.e. the derivation of rules of law for application in unregulated factual cases of "the nature of the matter" etc.

As noted, recent realist theories reject the concepts of justice and natural law, referring to their lack of objective existence and dependence on subjective judgements. Once "naïve realism" has been rejected, however, it is not meaningless to speak of justice and natural law as concepts reflecting universal human thought structures present throughout history and retaining their force of appeal for the acceptance of essential feelings and attitudes. Our feelings are, as we know, tied to the needs of our biological nature and our reactions to impressions. In this state we all belong to one animal species with identical physical and psychological needs and demands on our surroundings, and it is not surprising that from ancient times, people have felt that they shared the same "social needs", i.e. natural demands on the social organisation. The oldest theories are cosmic and divine and see the world order as governed by divine powers which also control human fate. The so-called Sophists of old Athens were the first to argue for the freedom of people, unhampered by divine powers, to organise society arbitrarily through a contract. This contract in turn presupposed democratic powers in the making of "political" decisions, and that also includes in our sense of the term most legal decisions made by the people's assembly.

Following the collapse of democracy, Aristotle formulated his theory of man's "social nature", which disposes us to organise society in a rational manner in order to create "the good life". Aristotle also founded the theory of justice, which he separated into commutative and distributive justice, of which the former was the older, while the latter was linked to the formation of the city state. The theory of man's social nature was given a principle of "equality" by the Stoics and a notion of the inherent value of each individual as a participant in divine reason. In combination with Christian individualism, natural law penetrated to Rome where it was formulated in three precepts: (1) live honestly, (2) do not harm others, and (3) give others their due.

During the time of the Crusades, the first Catholic church rejected the idea of man's inherent "goodness" and, based on contemporary experiences, the Church appealed to the inscrutable will of God to chastise sinful man into submission. In the height of the Medieval period after the rediscovery of Aristotle's writings, the theory of man's social nature was revived. We must of course respect the laws of God, but also those principles of natural law which are in harmony with our nature. These principles could be supplemented by positive secular legislation. Right of reaction exists only in connection with laws which go against the will of God.

The moral philosophy of the Church developed and expanded this social theory and the concept of justice especially in the sense of "just retribution" and "just payment". Maximum prices and a prohibition against usury were a fixed part of canon law. This theory was further elaborated by Grotius and transformed into a secular theory of moral or natural law based in a general theory of contract, which was continued by Samuel Pufendorf and other German writers, while at the same time, Thomas Hobbes' pessimistic view of human nature led him in the interest of peace to restrict the significance of the social contract to an agreement to leave all sovereignty to the king.

Since then a schism has existed between a Catholic perception of man and society, which favours minimal legislation, and a Protestant perception, which, with roots in Luther's adoption of St. Augustine's view of man, favours a greater degree of legislative control. In return, and according to Calvin, people have some degree of liberty to resist "unjust" laws in general.

More recently during the post-war years, the German philosophy of law in particular turned to natural law in consequence of the claim that legal positivism had been the reason why lawyers had not "resisted" the suppression of human rights during the Nazi regime. Such substantive theories of natural law are, however, difficult to defend, as it has not been possible since the critiques of Hume and Kant around 1800 to operate with a "universal reason" which grants us objective insight into eternal and immutable values. It has also been argued that it ought not be possible to legitimise a former irrational theory of law indirectly through criticism of a "rational" theory based on reference to a new irrationality.

More recently, however, attempts have been made to justify a new natural law theory by empirical means. Inspiration has been sought in ethology or animal psychology, and ethnology, the study of primitive societies, in order to find inspiration for "deductions" from our biological nature. When it is recognised that it is in principle impossible to derive a normative natural law from empirical facts and similarly recognised that the faculty of reason liberates human beings from dependency on their surroundings and turns them into makers of culture, there is no harm in seeking inspiration in these sciences for a theory of the "right" society (natural law as social theory). The theory may, however, be adjusted through the political process which is the experimental arena of society.

Political ideologies must, however, take their basis in a perception of human nature. Are we collective beings with a need for safety, as socialists and conservatives argue, or are we individuals with a need for freedom, as the liberalists claim? That we must by necessity live in a society and therefore must be "social beings" is evident, as the newborn is helpless for many years, but nothing factual can be derived from this circumstance about the organisation of the society. From the time of the oldest constitutions up to present times, we do, however, find a "minimum content of law" as pointed out by Hart. This law is the demand for truth and protection of personal and material integrity: thou shalt not lie, thou shalt not steal, thou shalt not kill! The Christian commandment of love only comes later.

These demands and others: the publication of the law and prohibition against retroactive force, understandability, ability and interconnection between rule and behaviour are conditions on which society depends for its functioning (Lon Fuller, *The Morality of Law*, 2nd. ed. 1969, Ch. 3).

However this may be, it is impossible to hold a qualified opinion about the social order and the organisation and function of the legal system without a view of human nature based on the dual need of freedom and safety. Similarly, as we are forced to accept a concept of natural law as a structural concept with mutable content, we must be able to speak of justice as one of the universal human thought structures. Its formal structure is identical with its rule structure: like cases must be treated alike! Its material structure contains an idea about one or other form of equality both in regard to reciprocity and in regard to the treatment of the individual perceived with varying degrees of inclusiveness. The "socially created" or distributive justice must, in common with the natural law concept, be of mutable content and dependent on the culture of the society.

Recent developments in Eastern Europe have served to deny the socialist, *Marxist* myth that the good society would develop as a result of the abolition of the right of private property. Quite the contrary, it has been found that the takeover by the state of the means of production has led to a totalitarian society in which the "rights" of the individuals have been subjected to the interests of the state. In return, the liberalistic myth that the good society is the result of the *pact*, the social contract, which reduces the influence of the state to a minimum, has shown tendencies to create chaos or anarchy.

While Marx saw power as the outcome of economic forces originating in the selfish exploitation of the right to own the means of production, Liberalism has seen power as the outcome of the state's suppression of the freedom of the individuals. Neo-Marxist theories as expressed by Habermas and Teubner seek to solve the dilemma of socialism by uniting the economic and political perspective and combining economic and political powers with equality and freedom through "communication" or "discourse". Behind these ideas we find in fact an adoption of a "grassroots" system (participation) which delegates the decisions to the social interests involved.

Such a model was attempted in Yugoslavia, where the means of production were given to the workers for autonomous administration. The result was unfortunate in that individual firms paid all their profits in wages to their employees, with the result that necessary investments were neglected, as were the interests of "society". In the first instance, local party control was introduced in order to solve this dilemma, but as this failed to achieve consideration of regional interests, regional control was then introduced and later again federal control.

The total result of this experiment in "communication" was unsatisfactory, as it failed to solve the need for both efficiency and freedom. Experiences gained from the testing of "grassroots" models in Denmark, namely in tertiary educational institutions, have similarly shown the fallacy of expecting local and "internal" interests to consider "external" or social interests. Neither has the Danish cooperative movement, which was partly based on similar ideas, been able to withstand competition from the "capitalist" market.

The reasons for these failures must be sought in the "idealistic" supposition underpinning the "democratic" theory of the Enlightenment, namely that political decisions are the outcome of a "rational debate among enlightened persons". A similarly "idealistic" assumption underlay the economic liberalism founded by Adam Smith (1723-90). When Adam Smith was able to believe that the selfish strivings of individual people would benefit society, it was because he also believed in "an invisible hand". Recent research has found that this theory was an influence from the rationalist natural law theory and its belief in man's social nature, *zoon politicon*.

Developments in the late 19th century gave the lie to both these assumptions, however, making it clear that political decisions are not the result of "rational debate" but a "struggle between interests", and that the rules of law form the battleground. Human beings are not only, and perhaps not even primarily, rational beings or social beings. Any social theory based on these assumptions ends in tyranny or anarchy, the former by its suppression of consciousness of human interests, the latter by its suppression of consciousness of human egotism.

In the name of social liberalism, Protestant countries have built a third model, the "welfare state", for the purpose of which, based on market economics and a belief in the ability of the law to control society, an administrative legislation of considerable scope and a corresponding bureaucracy has been established for the "equal" distribution of the fruits of society. Experience has also shown here that "public" and "private" powers have formed alliances and established so-called mixed "corporations" which have exercised actual social power in disregard of the interests of society and the "rights" of its individual members. The aim of the so-called "privatisation policy" was primarily to introduce mechanisms to ensure that public institutions and corporations see it as in their own interest to pay regard to the interests of society and "external" persons. Thus the proposal to leave the responsibility for the financing and administration of unemployment benefits to the labour market parties is an attempt to motivate the trade organisations to agree on a level of wages which will limit unemployment as much as possible.

The safest course is to assume that people are both selfish and altruistic, and are led by both reason and interests. The market economy is therefore the best agent for the simultaneous safeguarding of efficiency and freedom (commutative justice), and legislation for the safeguarding of equality and social morality (distributive justice). Tax legislation must be constructed with a view to the most efficient financing of the public sector, while the purpose of social law is in the broadest sense the possibility of establishing the greatest possible "welfare". Time has overtaken the "integrated" models, e.g. "social democracy", which aims at solving all fundamental problems through state control of economic operations on the basis of moral principles, tax policy on the basis of "inequality" (progression), and welfare policy on the basis of public institutions which may well distribute welfare according to need, but consider this a means rather than an end of the institution.

Just as grassroots control systems favour "local" (internal) interests at the cost of the whole, the "bureaucratic" model favours the interests of the bureaucracy at the cost of the interests of its "clients" or "society". People are both selfish and rational and will on the one hand maximise the advantages of the control system as opportunity offers, and on the other hand, through increasing social pressure, short circuit the various parts of the control systems.

"Civil disobedience" and "right of reaction" constitute a risk of the collapse of the legal and social system if enough people lose their faith in the system and their fear of sanctions. In that case a revolutionary situation arises, as in the "civil revolts" in the East, the growth of the "black economy", and disrespect for other parts of the control rules.

It has always been recognised that the rules of law cannot oblige anybody to do the impossible — *impossibillia nullum est obligatio* — and this includes things for which sanctions cannot or should not be introduced. On the other hand, it is not the suppression *per se* which gives rise to revolt, but the feeling of "injustice", said Thucydides (c. 456-396 BC).

CONCLUSIONS

The conclusion of the previous discussion must be that we must hold fast to the realist theory of knowledge which stipulates that reality exists prior to and independently of our knowledge of it. If we do not do this, we will lose the connection to and control of the realities, and end like earlier theories of law in purely academic speculations and automatic deductions from empty systems of concepts. True, it is important to construct clear and accurate concepts capable of serving as finely tuned tools for the legal technique, but precisely the fact that they are tools makes it necessary to adapt them to the solving of practical tasks.

The moot point in a realistic theory of knowledge remains, however, the transformation of sensory experience into language concepts. When we accept the proposition that reality is not "rational" because it is not structured *a priori* in a logical form and in language, we must "qualify" these sensory impressions in language, which represents reality as processed by consciousness. We start from the proposition that thought and language are two sides of the same coin, as the basis of both is concepts, i.e. formal structures which isolate certain conceptual elements from infinite reality, thus making it possible through this generalisation to find "the immutable in the mutable". By thus dividing reality into fractions and perspectives, we reduce it to formal relations, but we also make it predictable.

Consciousness operates with two types of concepts: the universal, which is clearly defined as the number and relations of its conceptual elements contain no ambiguity, and the type, which merely indicates its conceptual elements with no indication of precise numbers and relations. Universals are especially suited to scientific purposes as they allow definite and rapid deductions, while types are well suited to the less precise, but "meaningful", purposes of daily language use. Language therefore has a "redundancy of meaning" which makes it possible to function with a limited number of words. In return, individual words are open to "interpretation", as they have several meanings depending on syntax and context.

We have proceeded on the basis that this property of language supports the view that our experiences are made "understandable" through comparison with concepts we already know, thus allowing new experiences to be allocated through analogy to the concept which we find them most like. Our experience is thus primarily inductive, but this does not mean that language is a conventional sign system, rather that it depends on a universal "language competence" involving both a deep and a surface structure and which, because it is part of our sensory apparatus, must be "useful", i.e. capable of application to reality.

Although language competence is thus a part of our total cognitive apparatus and therewith dependent on "biological" and "intuitive" processes, it is not enough to refer the whole language qualification process to intuition or common sense, as this would place language use — and thus science — outside rational control. While science must respect the principle of reality, it may not ignore the principle of reason.

A realistic theory of law cannot, as in Alf Ross's theory, proceed on the assumption that legal science propositions are capable of verification, i.e. demonstrate phenomena in the world around us which correspond objectively to the content of the proposition (have "semantic reference"). It is not possible to describe reality in an objective language, and it is therefore not possible, as Ross does, to distinguish sharply between description and evaluation. This circumstance is emphasised by the fact that legal language must perforce be expressed in everyday words and concepts, as the purpose of the law is to influence social reality. The language of the law must therefore predominantly use type concepts which are open to interpretation. When the typical meaning is to be decided, one must perforce seek guidance in the purposes embedded in the rule, whether consciously or unconsciously, and compare with the practical effects to which the various interpretations would lead. Teleological and pragmatic elements must therefore perforce enter into the legal interpretation and the legal qualification of facts, which are two sides of the same coin.

If it is understood that the science of law in its traditional form, the dogmatic, is a practical and interpretative science and not a theoretical and descriptive science, it is clear, on the other hand, that there is no difference in principle in the interpretation of the sources of law and the application of law. The former activity fleshes out the general rules in hypothetical typical cases, the other qualifies factual cases in terms of legal concepts within a normative system. The dogmatic interpretation and the legal deduction are merely the conclusion of a psychological motivational process, comprising evaluations and analogies, which is justified in the form of a language syllogism which demonstrates that it is possible to fit the case into the normative system.

Jurisprudence is thus a practical and interpretative science, a quality which it shares with the arts and with theology. Jurisprudence is also a social science, as its interpretations are in part normative and in part concern the intended effect on reality. The study of law cannot, therefore, be separated from reality, neither the historical, the cultural, the ideological nor the political reality, as reality forms the basis of the interpretation and description which is the aim in its broadest sense of the study of law and the application of law. Reality is the total "conceptual horizon". Within specific areas of law, one must take one's basis in the legal principles underlying the individual law institutions, and by description and application of the law one must proceed from those general principles which govern western civilisation: individualism, private autonomy, democracy, rule of law, justice and fairness.

One consequence of our rejection of the logical empiricism is the fact that it again becomes possible to use the concept of "justice". From antiquity this concept has dominated the philosophy of law and morals. Justice has always had a definite logical structure, but different content depending on the historical reality. We can use the concepts "equity" and "fairness" in the same manner as expressions of the insight, known since antiquity, that the application of general rules always entails problems in individual delimitations, "*summum ius summa injuria*".

Jurisprudence is thus not "constructive" in the sense that it exclusively uses rational and logical methods. Neither is its task, therefore, merely to apply the principles which govern a law institute as a whole in the solving of practical detailed issues. The "general principles" or the "ideas" which govern the rationalist natural theory and the jurisprudence of concepts are not adequate tools for the study of law, which must include considerations of the demands and risks of the external world. This must be done on the basis of teleological and pragmatic considerations seen in relation to the demand for the rule of law, which constitutes a fundamental value in law, based as it is on foreseeability, and the demand for formal justice, which dictates that like cases must be treated alike on the basis of a general rule.

The subsidiary source of law is therefore "the nature of things", which aims at settling actual conflicts on the basis of actual justice, but such that the decision may serve as a model for future decisions. This is also why, in practical terms, legal usage is an important "source of law". The study of law is also an important guide for legal usage, provided it does not satisfy itself by systematic registering, but undertakes the construction of new models and patterns for future problem solutions based on the total experience, theoretical as well as practical, of contemporary life. If, following this route, jurisprudence becomes "creative", it is a creativity which presupposes a theoretical analysis, a conscious awareness of philosophy, ideology and factual situations, if it is not to degenerate into a non-principled and non-theoretical realism.

Just as science is bound at any given time by the sum of its own experiences, conditions, and limitations in its insight, jurisprudence is bound and tied at any given time to contemporary general science, its directions and methods, and hence also to its terminology. At any given time, therefore, the scientific truth is determined by the best insight of the science and the consensus view among its practitioners. The science of law is thus also "pragmatic", as the criterion of truth depends on the extent of the practitioners' experience and understanding. Hence theories of law are generally tied to the most current problems of the time, which are therefore made the object of the scientific criterion. It follows that the functions of law, codifying, conflict resolution and control, most often serve as the model or analogy for the philosophy of law and the theory of law. Custom becomes the most important model for pre-state societies, the command theory for despotic states, the contract model for liberal states, and the control model for the welfare state. In the pluralistic society of our time we accept pluralistic models of legal theory. We accept that there are other sciences of law than the dogmatic, and that these latter sciences, the "comparative" (history of law, comparative law), sociological (legal sociology) and political (politics of law) must use other methods than dogmatism.

The dogmatic study of law is an old science, the roots of which go back to the rhetorical and interpretative science of antiquity. It is both specific and general, in so far as it not only analyses and systematises principles and arguments for the solving of factual cases in law, but also stresses the need for the application of rules in this task. Compared with the generalising process of the natural sciences, which formulate experiences in laws of causation, the science of law stresses the importance of generalisations in the form of normative laws. Compared with the forward-looking evaluations of consequences of the social sciences, the law of science stresses the importance of backward-looking normative evaluations.

Confronted with the functional reasoning of the social sciences, the science of law will stress the function of law as an important factor in the planning and administration of the interests of society. Faced with the legal, economic and other "reflexive" systems theories, it must be argued that economic rationality — and this applies to both the market economic and the social economic model — is not the only type of rationality, and that interests involving the rule of law and other values can lead to solutions of social problems which depart from economic efficiency, which cannot, therefore, serve as the exclusive model of the argumentation of jurisprudence either. As against the general legal sociological systems theories it is important to insist on the normative element in law versus any systems adaptation, as other concerns in the form of ideological or moral principles may be cited in support of the law's normative element. One may, for example, uphold a prohibition against euthanasia for reasons of principle, although this stand cannot be rationalised through economic or other reasons of efficiency.

It is hard to say what consequences it may have for legal

dogmatism and legal usage that the interpretation of legal material and the description of legal facts may now be given equal weight. The current development in recent legal usage does, however, indicate a greater sense of freedom in the choice and weighting of arguments together with a more open and explicit application of normative and pragmatic arguments.

Part 2

Justice

In general, it appears that it angers people more to be wronged than coerced, for the former is considered unfair treatment by an equal, but the latter as force by a superior.

Thucydides (460-400 BC)

INTRODUCTION

"Justice" means that people get what they deserve.

In primitive societies, where life is lived collectively and objectively, this means that the allocation of values follows status relations, that payment must correspond to services rendered and retribution to the evil perpetrated. Generally, it is the gods who decide the fate of people in life and thus the lot they are allocated.

In organised societies, people's just desserts are determined by their contributions and hence by their value to the community. In developed societies with an individualistic and subjective way of life, just desserts are determined by good or evil intent.

This does not, of course, imply that a single type of just dessert applies to any given way of life, but rather that the various types supplement one another and apply to different sectors and in different situations side by side. In *private law*, justice with regard to service rendered is the main factor in determining the legal relationship, as the purpose in general is to obtain a balance between service and payment. If the balance shifts, various forms of legal redress are available for maintaining a reasonable balance. In Denmark, the most general means is Section 36 of the Danish Contract Act, which enables the courts to overrule "unreasonable" contractual terms, while the law of obligation also contains legal means enabling partial or full cancellation if a significant imbalance is found to exist or to arise between the services rendered by the parties. These rules go back to the rationalist natural law, which adopted them from the Catholic moral philosophy dogma concerning "just payment" or *justum pretium*, which in turn goes back to Aristotle's metaphysics and ethics.

In *criminal law*, objective retribution under influence of the Christian dogma of guilt has been replaced by a form of retribution dependent on and measured by the degree of evil intent or *culpa*. Compensation law, which represents the old system of retribution aimed at redressing the loss suffered by the injured party, is similarly dominated in general by an ordinary rule of *culpa*, while the level of retribution or compensation is fixed in proportion to the loss suffered. Just as retribution under private law may sometimes depend on subjective conditions or *culpa*, legal retribution under both compensation law and criminal law may be tied to purely objective actions, although in the interest of the rule of law this is less common.

Justice is not, however, merely tied to the result of the balancing of service against merit, but also to the *procedure* under which the best and most efficacious rendering of justice may be achieved.

From time immemorial, the scales have been the symbol of justice, literally weighing service against payment, just dessert against reward or punishment. In the course of legal development, procedures have gradually been established, each of which in its own time constituted a fair trial for establishing the rights and wrongs of a case. It is not much good being in the right if one cannot have one's rights.

In one form or another, the notion has always existed that life should be just and that reward and punishment should be awarded accordingly. It has therefore been important for people to find an explanation, or rather a justification, of good or bad fortune in the form of good deeds or bad deeds. Death, disease, crop failure or war must be due to an offence to the gods who are appeased by sacrifices or penitence. Through prayer or rituals, one seeks to keep misfortune at bay.

Human beings have based their lives on the notion in various shapes and forms that their actions or failures to act are the reason for their positive or negative circumstances in life. The whole faith in progress is based on the assumption that God helps him who helps himself, and that the cause of progress and misfortune lies within oneself. When deciding on eternal salvation, God looks at intention and disposition. Justification through faith is one of the fundamental Christian, and especially Protestant, dogmas.

The thesis of Part 2 of this book is thus the claim that the notion of justice has its roots in a primary human need to believe that life, both on this side of the grave and beyond, ensures a certain balance between our actions, their motivations and consequences, that things happen according to merit and by just dessert. This part of morality is essential for the law, and it has constituted a fundamental problem for the study of law ever since law became divorced from morality as a result of our forefathers' abandoning of their faith in divinely sanctioned custom in favour of a belief in the human power of legislation.

CONCEPT AND HISTORY

Justice is both a legal philosophical and a theological concept. The following account will be restricted largely to its application and meaning in jurisdiction and the history of law.

In positivist theory of law the concept was banned as meaningless, while in more recent theories and applications of the law it has again become possible to use arguments referring to questions of just or reasonable resolutions.

The concept of justice exists in several different variations, two of the most common of which go back to Aristotle's ethics: corrective justice and distributive justice; but they may possibly be united in the Stoic doctrine of *(ta aisima) "suum"*, "give unto every man that which is his". The Roman concepts *justitia* and *aequitas* refer to custom and equilibrium, which in turn go back to ancient Egyptian notions of the scales as the symbol of law while pointing forward to Medieval ethics and rationalist natural law theory of the 1600s and 1700s.

The idealist school of thought of the 1800s continued to see value judgements, including justice, as objects of scientific knowledge, but the anti-idealist theories of the 20th century denied justice. The question is whether and how the concept of justice is capable of rehabilitation.

In the same manner as morality and ethics, *justitia* in the Roman and *epieikeia* in the Greek language refer to custom and to the need to act in the customary manner, according to a rule, as do also the Germanic words for *law* and *justice*. The primitive concept of law is that it constitutes divine custom, as the Church also approved custom in Europe in the Middle Ages.

Justice can be rule-oriented and process-oriented. *Rule*-oriented justice is an expression of the formal tenet of justice, known as Kant's golden rule, that like cases must be treated alike. *Process*-oriented justice is an expression of *due process* or fair trial. Process guarantees ensure just decisions. They are particularly widespread in Anglo-Saxon legal and moral philosophy as represented by John Rawls (b. 1921) and Ronald Dworkin, with the judge occupying an exalted position in Anglo-Saxon tradition.

A third form of justice is *equity*, in Greek *epieikeia*, that which is fair and right, in Latin, *aequum et bonum, aequita*, in German, *Treu und Glauben*, in Danish *rimelighed*. It has always been clear that custom should be administered with reason. Plato and Aristotle later expressed the thought that application of an abstract rule requires *specification*. This is because the abstraction represents an induction from actual typical social situations which allow the abstract formulation to "cover" more, i.e. to have competence to cover situations not yet arisen or foreseen. The abstraction thus has a "generative" competence, and it follows that a mechanism is required for separating out meanings which are in conflict with the purpose, intentions and pragmatism of the rule. On the other hand, the limit of the formulation of the rule is normally also the limit of its application, unless "causal similarity" leads to an *analogy* being drawn by application of a higher principle. The dictates of the rule of law must be placed against equity on the scales of justice.

Law and right are near synonyms, as are other rhetorical terms such as joy and happiness etc. The word "law", in Danish *lov*, derives from that which has been "laid down" or fixed, i.e. the customary. The word goes back to the earliest north Germanic language and originally meant *layer* or *stratum*, but it is related to the Latin *lex*, from *ligo*, i.e. to fasten or bind, in Greek *legein*, i.e. to lay or write. The original meaning of the word "right", German *Recht*, French *droit*, is "straight", in contrast to "bent", i.e. that which follows a straight line is controlling or directional. Neither was there originally any distinction between the actual decision and the abstract rule. We find the same near-synonymous meaning in the rhetorical terms "law and judgement" and "law and justice". "Justice" means to do what is right, to be a person who does what is right, to act in accordance with what is right.

There is no question that justice in this *formal* sense of the word constitutes a fixed component in a concept of justice, in the same manner as "right" constitutes a fixed contrast to "wrong", i.e. to arbitrariness or power, while any *substantive* concept of justice must be relative, i.e. it must depend on the state of law in any given period or any given place. In any absolute sense, the terms justice and natural law can at most contain some general principles seen as a precondition for the existence of society, the minimum content of law: you must not lie, you must respect the integrity of the person and property of others; but other moral principles are also claimed in canon law and in Lon Fuller's (1902-78) work: laws must be promulgated, they may not be retrospective, they may not demand what is impossible, they must be possible to understand and not self-contradictory or the object of frequent change, and of course they must be obeyed.

Primitive societies are collective and oriented towards the family, while modern society is individualistic. The difference is therefore that in the former case the law is objective and casuistic, while in the latter it is subjective and general. In any substantive sense, therefore, justice must vary in step with society's political and ideological content, but societies at the same level of development appear to face the same problems and to solve them in similar ways, despite apparent differences in the formulation of rules due to different traditions and organisational forms. It is particularly this *necessary* difference in substantive content which has led to the rejection of the concept of justice, but there is no reason why justice should not be considered a logical structure with changing content, a "dynamic natural law" or a natural law with changing content. As Thucydides wrote of the Peloponnesian War, people will bear great suffering with fortitude, but if treated unjustly, they become rebellious.

JUSTICE AND EQUALITY

Equality may be defined in various ways depending on the criteria applied:

1. Service for service
2. Like cases are treated alike
3. All human beings are treated alike
4. Equal opportunities for all
5. a)   Equal pay for equal work
   b)   Equal pay for men and women
   c)   Equal pay for all (serve according to ability and receive according to need, universal pay).

Justice is thus tied to equality, first and foremost in the meaning of (2) above, that all like cases should be treated alike. It is not only the formal rule which must cover all "like" cases, but also the enforcement which must be equal. It also enters into Lon Fuller's moral requirement of the legal system that rule and behaviour must accord.

The ideal situation is where the rule corresponds to morality and everybody consequently follows the rule spontaneously. The most important function of the legal and social structure since the early Medieval period has been "peace and justice", *pax et justitia*. The doctrine of the two swords, the ecclesiastic and the secular, goes back to St. Augustine. It is the duty of the prince to support right with might, as it has been known since antiquity (Aristotle) that right without might is no more than good advice, and St. Augustine held that since the Fall, man must be chastised into obedience. But it is clear from canon law (cf. the preamble to the Danish regional law), *Jydske Lov*, that it is the duty of the king to protect the people of the Church, widows, and the fatherless who lack family protection.

In post-Socratic philosophy the law was given a moral and reasonable content. Aristotle held that man is both a rational and a social being, *zoon politicon*, and that a special natural law disposed human beings to do what is good, and what is good may be known only through reason. This theory reappeared in the height of the Medieval period, when Aristotle's ethics and politics were rediscovered in the west, and in *Summa Theologica*, Thomas Aquinas developed a theory of the tripartite division of law: God's law, natural law and positive law. Two lines depart from Thomas Aquinas: (1) a new natural law leading from a basis in man's social nature through the Catholic moral philosophy and the rationalist natural law of the 1600s and 1700s to the philosophy of the Enlightenment, and (2) a positivist theory of legislation according to which natural law consists of principles to be filled in by the prince, who must be obeyed also if his law is in conflict with natural law. Only if his law conflicts with the law of God do the people have a "right" to resist the law. This legal positivism was further developed in the 1300s and 1400s, culminating with Machiavelli in the 1500s and Thomas Hobbes in the 1600s, the "social contract" which makes Grotius argue in favour of government by the people, for Hobbes comes to mean an agreement to transfer sovereignty to the prince (cf. the Danish Law of King Christian V).

Theoretical Marxism similarly assumed that people are social beings and will therefore act "rightly" if suppression ceases through the abolition of capitalism. In the communist society, the law will wither and ultimately die. Reality in actually existing socialist states was, as we know, different. St. Augustine was right. We do not auto-matically obey the law, and it must therefore be enforced unless one "legalises" transgressions by adapting the law to life as we live it.

In their administration of the law, the authorities must therefore act equitably, and the existence of a principle of equality has indeed also been postulated in recent administrative law. Breaches must likewise be handled equitably, as nobody will tolerate limitations in their freedom unless others are forced to tolerate similar limitations. In extreme cases, anarchy will follow if the law is not enforced. We know the problem today from "inflation" in the law, especially from regulations under administrative law, and we have seen attempts at "deregulation" in order to ensure both efficacy and justice. In Danish society, tax planning, tax evasion and smuggling have become approved sports, in contrast to theft, violence and similar activities.

We conclude that justice is a meaningful term in the sense that it has been used as a logical structure in the most ancient cultures for the naming of an action or dealing which is "just" or "deserved".

EQUALITY OR ARBITRARINESS

Formal justice or *isonomia*, in contrast to arbitrariness or *cadi justice*, is a central element in the concept of justice. Like cases must be treated alike.

Substantive justice is more ambiguous as it changes with culture. *Corrective* or proportional justice does, however, also appear to be an original and constant value. From the time of the earliest Egyptian culture, the scales have been the symbol of justice, *Lady Justitia*. In pre-state societies, the "criminal law" is part of private law. This is why revenge was replaced by a *talion* or composition system, whereby retribution was limited to revenge in like measure or a "proportionate" penalty. In religious terms, God's punishment is a consequence of human sin, and it may be prevented through prayer or sacrifice. In contract law a similar principle of just retribution applies, called variously *synallagma, quid pro quo* or *justum pretium*. In all matters, people must be treated according to just desserts, and every man must be paid his due, *suum*.

With the development of urban societies, the strong family ties dissolved and it became possible for "central government" to reward citizens according to their value to society in accordance with *distributive* justice, in aristocratic societies according to merit, in democratic societies equitably. In the Greek-Christian culture culminating in western Europe in the Renaissance and the Enlightenment, the individualist ideology developed which led to the Human Rights Declaration of 1789: human beings are free and equal. Kant gave a radical formulation of the concept of freedom and gave the state the authority to regulate its citizens' equal rights to freedom. Individual citizens were enclosed in an inviolable legal sphere, capable of delimitation only through *judicial* procedures in accordance with general principles of procedure, which were openness, contradiction, presumption of innocence in favour of the accused, and rule of law, involving clear, published, fully enacted laws.

Corrective justice cannot be reduced to distributive justice or social utility. In a democratic society, the interest of individual freedom and the security of life and property normally rank more highly than social utility. Even John Rawls' social liberal *A Theory of Justice* recognises the fact that equality must give way to freedom if this will benefit the less privileged. Whether result- or rule-oriented, utilitarianism cannot cancel "justice". Justice must be considered part of rule utilitarianism. It is an independent and important social function; rules and institutions are given a higher priority than economy.

Rawls' theory of justice is thus an expression of a social liberal political ideology in harmony with individual freedom and social security (equality, welfare), while Robert Nozick's "minimum state" is an expression of the so-called "night watchman ideology" or the new liberalism which places weight on individual freedom and market economy (neo-classicism, monetarism) believing, as do the classical economic liberalism and utilitarianism, that the "invisible hand" ensures the public good.

Japanese culture does not know concepts such as "justice", "equity", "conscience" or "guilt", as Japanese society builds on collective responsibility. Indian culture is similarly without compassion. People have no individual value.

The concept of *fairness* applies to procedure, *justice* to the result of the procedure. But the western problem of justice is under all circumstances based on a fundamental individualism in contrast to the collectivism of Asia and Africa, where the individual person or the collective is the smallest unit of society.

The Danish *billighed*, that which is fitting, originally meant *actual justice* in the application of an abstract legal rule. The Roman *aequitas* rather means equality as fairness, as does the British *equity* and Section 36 of the Danish Contract Act, which says that unreasonable conditions may be overruled.

RULE — PRINCIPLE

H.L.A. Hart's (1907-92) legal positivism also rests on a moral theory: that it is good to have a legal system, and that such systems consist of *rules*. Hart makes a claim for: (1) "rules of recognition" which serve to identify valid law and to establish an *obligation* to act in accordance with rules, and that (2) rules are different from commands in being general. Inherent in this claim is a dual recognition of "justice", presupposing as it does both the rule of law and formal justice.

Dworkin's criticism of Hart's theory of law as a system of rules is based on the claim that the law consists of *principles* which form the basis of legal argumentation and political principles, firstly freedom, secondly equality and thirdly fair trial.

Dworkin's theory has not, in my view, been adequately analysed, but remains purely a legal theory and not a philosophical theory. Dworkin does not analyse the essential *teleological* element in language and hence in the legal rules, an element which does not allow interpretation of the language of the rules without taking into account the purposes built into concepts, institutions and rules. This means that one cannot interpret the language of the rules without taking into account the political, ideological and practical purposes of the rules. Referring to their language content in an *ordinary language sense*, it could be said that the rules of law are *not* exhaustive if one refers to their content in terms of *ordinary language* use (Hart), or that they are *always* exhaustive, in so far as *hard cases* may always be settled on the basis of moral principles (Dworkin). Both claims are inaccurate, in the former case because language does not *only* have an ordinary meaning (context, systematics, logic, semantics), but also a specific meaning (teleology, pragmatics). The *purpose* of legal rules is to influence actions. It is not, on the other hand, correct to say that only an "independent" decision may be made, either because the conflict solver holds an independent position as the law giver, or because he is free to use moral arguments. The argumentation will always be a *legal* argumentation as it must be undertaken within the framework of the teleological and pragmatic elements which inevitably exist in legal concepts, institutions and rules. This argumentation is called "legal method".

Underpinning our legal institutions is of course a political ideology, which in *private law* is called *"private autonomy"*, in *criminal law "in dubio pro reo"*, in *constitutional law "human rights"*, in *administrative law "the rule of law"* and *"the principle of equality"*.

MORALITY AND JUSTICE

Justice and morality are not the same thing, but justice must be part of morality in the original sense of the word, i.e. as that which is right or straight, the customary, in contrast to what is bent and arbitrary, and also in a later natural law sense, i.e. as morality's requirement of the law (the "right" society, *polis*) or in an individual sense (justice, rule of law and judicial procedures in contrast to administrative procedures or social opportunism).

"Justice" in the sense of a moral requirement of legislation emerges in post-Socratic social philosophy, expounded by Plato and Aristotle, who thought that Sophist legal positivism, i.e. democracy, makes conventional decisions and fails to distinguish between general laws and specific judgements. Plato and Aristotle saw the misfortunes suffered during the Peloponnesian War as caused by an immoral cynical and opportunistic attitude in the people's assembly, where arbitrary and heartless or contradictory decisions were taken. They thought, therefore, that laws should be general and moral in accordance with man's social and rational nature, a nature made to develop ideally in the *polis* or *politica*.

Later, Franz From (b. 1914) was to propose a connection between morality and reliability. The person who acted unreliably had acted immorally and carried the "blame" for any accident. A connection probably does exist between morality and reason in the sense that in an organised society, it is sensible to act in a moral manner, as any maximisation of immediate profit will lead to a break in useful relations. A psychopath only makes single deals.

Lon Fuller's eight "moral" requirements of the law probably constitute the most accurate conditions of efficacy of a community founded on law which we can establish.

1. The law must consist of rules
2. The rules must be publicised
3. The rules may not be retroactive
4. The rules must be understandable

5. The rules may not demand the impossible
6. The rules must not be subject to frequent changes
7. The rules must not be self-contradictory
8. There must be harmony between rule and behaviour

To this should be added Hart's "minimum content": truth (Sisela Bock), protection of the integrity of persons and property as well as acceptance by the majority.

Any moral and legal argumentation is *governed by rules*, in contrast to *instrumental* argumentation which is oriented towards consequences. The former looks backward towards a "cause" or "ground", the latter looks forward towards a consequence. It is not difficult to understand that a reference to a positive or negative consequence can constitute a convincing argument, *but why should a reference to a "cause" or "ground" be equally — or even more — convincing?* Why is it possible to justify, legitimise, a decision by referring to a rule, an ideology, a religion or an authority? Why do people allow themselves to be "convinced" by "grounds" which are not the same as "causes"? *Causes* "explain" an action, while *grounds* "excuse" or "justify" the action. Why does "justice" explain that somebody must be punished or pay compensation if they have harmed another? In modern times this attitude has been "rationalised" with reference to *prevention*. In recent centuries, the reason given by criminal law and compensation law is the interest in avoiding harm. The viewpoint has been shifted from a rule-bound backward-looking argumentation to a forward-looking pragmatic argumentation. With regard to the criminal law, the doubt of recent years in measures of general and special prevention has led to a neo-classical theory of punishment reintroducing the stress on just, i.e. proportionate, retribution. Those who were admitted to houses of correction or to other types of treatment considered the indefinite "punishment" unjust.

The closest one is likely to come to an answer is probably to see the convincing legitimising effect which argumentation based on rules and justice has as *inherent in and consequent upon human consciousness and as a consequence of the social need for order and peace. Pax et justitia* has always been society's ideal.

CONDITIONS OF VALIDITY OR FUNCTION

One thing which causes fundamental problems when analysing the relationship between law and morality or law and justice is the fact that it is difficult to distinguish between "conditions of validity" and "conditions of functionality". "Conditions of validity" means the criteria for establishing legal obligations; "conditions of functionality" means the conditions under which a society will be able to function. Some variations of the concept of natural law have the same content.

Normally when speaking of conditions of validity, a distinction is made between formal and substantive validity. "*Formal*" validity means that rules must derive from certain sources — legal sources — which ultimately derive from one or more legal source principles. The status and nature of this "ultimate source" has been the object of much dispute. Hans Kelsen, wanting to found a "pure" and "positive" theory of law in order to keep law free of abuse by totalitarian, political and religious ideologies and in order to argue in favour of a democratic constitutional state, identified law and state, defining law as the norms supported by the state's enforcement apparatus and thus derived from the state's constitutional system, which in turn is derived from a "basic norm". This basic norm, however, is no more than a logical presupposition, the sole purpose of which, as in all logical systems, is to legitimise the system and to cut off a process of infinite regression. Kelsen's theory is "pure" in the sense that it is purely analytical and has no connection with any specific society, its politics, behaviour or morality. In such an analytical positive system, this means that the concept of "justice" carries no authority.

While Kelsen wants to analyse and legitimise a legal system or rule of law, Hart's intention is to analyse the concept of law. Hart agrees with Kelsen on most points, but he cannot accept that the "basic norm" is an abstract norm void of content. Under the name *rule of recognition*, he ties it to a specific legal system and fastens it with a socio-psychological "popular" recognition of the "system". This makes the theory analytical, although as pointed out by Hart himself in the preface, it is a sociological theory of law, a fact supported by his claim that in order to function, any society (governed by law) must have a "minimum content" of morality: truthfulness, prohibition against violence, theft, etc.

Within these "conditions of functionality", Hart maintains that the theory of law must be a "positive theory", as morality or natural law cannot invalidate formally correctly established norms or legal acts. However immoral it may have been, the law of the Third Reich was thus not *"Unrecht als System"*, as the German jurist Gustav Radbruch (1878-1949) wrote after the war. It is clear from this that Hart cannot accept substantive, i.e. natural legal or moral conditions of validity which give people the "right" to disobey or resist the law.

The law, he says, consists of "duties" derived from the rule of recognition and not just from behaviour, and unlike sociology, jurisprudence does not consist of predictions of legal behaviour, as American and Scandinavian realism thought in the earlier half of this century. The law has not only an "external perspective" but also an "internal perspective". It cannot be viewed only from the perspective of the lawyer or legal sociologist. It is not much help for the judge to be told that the law is what the judge is actually doing, or predictions about what he may do.

The Danish legal philosopher Alf Ross attempted to unite Kelsen and Hart by combining Kelsen's identification of law and state, American realism's prognosis apparatus and Hart's "internal perspective". Ross did not want to analyse an abstract concept of law or a formal legal system, but to found a *realist science of law*. His intention was thus not the authenticity of the law but its validity. "Valid Danish law" is the object of his science. His objective is to establish by what criteria the science of law *verifies* claims of what is *"valid law"*. The foundation of his theory is logical empiricism, which states that science can only concern itself with two types of propositions: (1) logical or analytical, and (2) empirical or synthetic. Science cannot work with "metaphysical" propositions or value judgements as these have no "semantic reference", i.e. their language content cannot be compared to any empirical fact in the external world or derived from a logical system.

While it seems it can be quite unproblematic for the natural sciences to verify their claims, at any rate when "the external world" is identified with the readings of measuring equipment, it is difficult to verify sociological and legal science claims.

One thing is certain for Ross: the concept of justice has no semantic reference and is therefore meaningless, a point Ross stresses by calling it "nonsense", "banging the table", an "inaritculate expression" and "every man's whore". It is clear that these terms are not neutral scientific statements. Ross fought with passion against the older idealist theory (Frederik Vinding Kruse (1880-1963)) which saw "justice" as the very idea of the legal system and its realisation as the most important goal of the legal apparatus, but Ross used too big a gun, and the ghost moved with him. In order to find a base for "predictions" and "valid law" other than individual psychological circumstances, as the American "behaviourism" had done, Ross introduced a "shared ideology of judges" as legal source, i.e. "valid law" is identical with this ideology as it is expressed in the judges' *grounds* for their decisions. In their grounds, judges express what they "feel" bound by. Ross combined predictions of legal behaviour with the interpretation of a legal ideology.

Ross's theory runs into a string of fundamental difficulties. Firstly, the concept "shared ideology of judges" is a metaphysical concept as it has no "semantic reference". Secondly, one cannot be sure that the judge does not "polish up" his decision with false grounds, as Ross himself points out in connection with his claim of the unscientific nature of value judgements. Thirdly, logical empiricism presupposes the possibility of an objective description, and we cannot satisfy this supposition given what we know of the pragmatic nature of language and concepts.

The difficulty of "realist" theories is also that they end by turning into legal sociology, thus offering no guidance for the practice of law. The task of jurisprudence is the same as for other "practical" sciences, to guide the practising lawyer in his interpretation of the rules of law and their application in the solving of specific conflicts in law, but it follows that the task is also to avoid legal conflicts by establishing a systematic, and as far as possible exhaustive, account of "valid" or "applicable" law. In this function, the science of law cannot avoid using value judgements, as the description of the external world will always constitute an interpretation because of the hermeneutic-teleological nature of language. As the rules of law have a social function in terms of promoting a behaviour which complies with "political" goals, and as the language of the rules is perforce adjusted to the typical social situation which forms the prototype of the rule, specific cases must be settled through a "specification" of the general norm which will also entail a language "qualification" of the actual circumstances. For help in this qualification, guidance must be sought in the purpose of the rule and in an assessment of the potential consequences of any alternative interpretation. Jurists now refer to this as "factual considerations" and "practicability", while in earlier times reference was made to the "nature of the matter", "equity" and "fairness in the specific instance". It is also interesting to note that Danish judgements of the last 20 years show a growing number of arguments of this latter type used increasingly in specifying grounds. A regressive movement appears to be in progress among lawyers from "practicability" to "equity", from a "utilitarian" towards a "realist" theory in the sense that the necessity, and hence permissibility, of value judgements is recognised in the science and the practice of law, both of which apply the same "legal method", i.e. ranking of interests on the basis of the "rule of law" and "practicability".

As we saw, the American jurist Lon Fuller criticised the realist and analytical branches of positivist legal theories, listing eight ethical requirements of the legal system. Lon Fuller sees these ethical requirements as *conditions of functionality*, similar to Hart's "minimum content", rather than as conditions of validity, and the distance is therefore not as great as it would seem in polemic terms. When the American legal theorist Ronald Dworkin now reaps some fame for his criticism of Hart, he does so on a weaker philosophical basis.

PLURALISM AND LEGAL PRINCIPLES

It is true that Hart's "rule of recognition", like Kelsen's "basic norm", leads to the conclusion that the law is a closed and exhaustive system of rules with the consequence that some "hard cases" which fall outside the system are left to the (arbitrary, *political*) decision of the judge: cf. Section 1 of the Swiss book of statutes, which states that the judge must assume the role of law-giver when judging a case not regulated by the law. Dworkin claims, on the other hand, that there is always a "right" solution to "hard cases", as the legal system is supplemented by a set of *moral* principles from which judges seek support, which claim Dworkin then proceeds to demonstrate in an elaborate analysis of dissenting "opinions" in notorious cases.

Both views may be traced back to the same outdated perception of "ordinary language" as the expression of "common sense". There is no such thing as an "objective normative content", and as a criterion for the analysis of language, "common sense" constitutes no more than an intuitive factor. When the tool applied in the processing of the external world is a "hermeneutic" analysis of language combined with a "relational" perception of the process, legal interpretation loses its mystery, as it must perforce be based on the *legal* principles underpinning legal language. All rules of law have arisen in response to historical and comparative factors in a given culture and for the purpose of regulating various aspects of its social life. Originally, the law was purely "reflexive", as primitive pre-state societies have only a "private law", i.e. rules regulating relationships between individuals, while it is the task of the family to protect its members and ensure the necessary order which is considered an essential part of a collective in every respect. The law is custom, often a sacred custom; balance and retaliation or fines are the expression of justice, that is to say of law.

With the growth of urban civilisations and the formation of states, public law emerges. This law is based to a greater extent on a principle of authority and an evaluation of individual social merit, that is to say on distributive justice. As society becomes increasingly technological and individualistic, its position in the state is justified as a "democratic" system. Constitutional law now takes its basis in "human rights", and the *principle of equality* comes to dominate the constitution and administrative law, while interests focused on the rule of law come to dominate criminal law and procedural law. One cannot "interpret" or use these parts of the legal system without taking the whole cultural situation into consideration. The resulting interpretation is therefore neither purely "political" nor purely "moral". Given that the political and moral principles are built into the social and legal system, they *also become legal principles*, entering into the legal interpretation or argumentation as a matter of course. In practical terms, the problem is how far this process of interpretation may be taken, i.e. how far jurisprudence can go in its advice to courts, *sententia ferenda*, and where the point lies where one exceeds one's legal competence and begins to argue politically, giving advice to the legislature, *de lege ferenda*. On a couple of occasions the Danish Supreme Court has expressed itself on this subject, most directly in the so-called "Christiania Case", where the court found that the decision whether "Free State Christiania" constituted a "social experiment" was an issue for parliament and not for the courts to decide. Being appointed and not elected by the people, courts have no political mandate. Under Section 3 of the Danish Constitution, the courts must "follow the law", and thus not make new law. Of course courts do in principle make new law through their decisions, as these impart specific content to general norms, and courts in federal states, such as the USA and Germany do, of course, hold more extensive "political" powers, as they must harmonise the legislation of independent states under the common constitution, but the fundamental division of powers between the production of general rules and the production of specific decisions must of course continue to apply.

It must also be argued against the analytical theories of law that they presuppose a monocentric law derived from a single source, and this is unrealistic. In modern times, legislation is an important source, especially with regard to administration law and public law including the constitution, criminal law and procedural law, but *private law* remains based on private autonomy and continues to be made through the statutes of organisations, company charters, general and specific contract terms and collective bargainings. This part of the law derived from such multifaceted sources constitutes by far the dominant part of the total volume of legal rules, and in cases of conflict, problem resolution is entrusted to private arbitration, industrial courts, vested in principal agreements or commercial courts according to general and specific contract terms. Large parts of compensation law and property law etc. have developed through legal custom.

The law is thus *polycentric*, and not monocentric or "systematic", as was the general view during the last century in many countries with general codifications. The ideal is of course that the law should be systematic, in order to avoid contradictory rules as far as possible, as this would not be compatible with "justice" (cf. Fuller above). But it is actually possible to live with a considerable level of inconsistency, exactly because of the polycentric nature of the law, just as it is possible to live with a high level of discrepancy between rule and behaviour, although, as noted, "justice" sets a limit for this tolerance.

"Justice" is a concept with many meanings, but common to all justice arguments is that they appear to contain an appeal for a kind of "equality", albeit equality in many forms. When statements are made to the effect that an advantage or disadvantage is "undeserved", as often happens, the underlying equality is corrective, involving the relationship of service to payment or crime to punishment. Other statements refer to equality in the form of equality with other persons, either in the form of equality under the law or equal treatment of all people. In the former case, the argument expresses criticism of the fact that others are not made responsible, or do not incur punishment when the person expressing the criticism was forced to suffer sanctions for the infringement or offence. As Thucydides said, people will put up with much misfortune, but not with injustice imposed by authorities. Arbitrariness or cadi justice is an intolerable form of "injustice".

The Aristotelian concept of equality does not go beyond this: that like cases should be treated alike, as people vary with regard to status and hence value. Society must reward its citizens relative to another concept of equality: distributive justice or just dessert. This aristocratic concept of justice as payment according to merit can take the form of payment according to status or payment according to effort. The former sense corresponds to the agrarian society with a barter economy while the latter belongs to urbanised societies with division of labour and a money economy. Within this social development, the concept of justice must develop such that the strong are forced to help the weak: the old and children who are no longer protected by family or gain a share of the common yield.

The Old Testament reflects the old agrarian tribal societies with revenge and *talion* (an eye for an eye) partially replaced by fines and the family's care of the old, who hold positions of high status, as experience is valued highly in static societies, and of children who represent future maintenance, making it a matter of prestige and riches to have many children, especially boys. Precisely this tradition contributes to preventing a modernisation of, especially, African and Asian societies as population growth prevents economic growth, confirming suspicions of the ability of society to maintain its people. This is a vicious circle, which western European cultures overcame with the individualisation of the Renaissance and the understanding that both physical and social surroundings can be changed by individuals. At the same time, population figures were kept in control relative to economic possibilities, but it was a slow process difficult to implant into traditional cultures unable to regulate birth numbers by either natural or artificial means.

With its radical individualism, the New Testament represents the new mentality. Individual persons are only responsible if they are "guilty", that is if they had an evil intent. People must not revenge themselves on their offenders, but turn the other cheek. Revenge is Caesar's or God's. Caesar, i.e. society, is responsible for and has the competence to keep peace and order, and God judges all living and dead on the last day, weighing them on the scales of sin and salvation like the old Egyptians. All human beings are our "neighbours"; we must love our neighbour as we love ourselves, especially the sick, the old and the young who especially are surrounded by the love of God.

This radical individualism harmonises with the Stoic dogma of man's divine equality as sharer in the eternal reason. It is this Stoic-Jewish/Christian individualism, with its insistence on the equality of all people, which later during the Renaissance and Enlightenment led to human rights and democracy. This represents the legitimisation of political equality in competition with other concepts of equality, service for service and punishment and reward by just dessert. *Suum cuique tribuitur!* To each according to *his* just dessert was the Stoic-Roman principle of justice supplemented with the legal *aequitas* aimed at ensuring equity and fairness in all legal matters.

In our time, the concept of justice remains tied to the concept or concepts of equality. For as Erik Rasmussen (1915-95) correctly points out in his work on concepts of equality, there are several competing concepts of equality. When wage claims are supported with reference to justice, the various equality concepts are applied in turn: statements are made about "equal pay for equal work", and "equal pay for all". The former of these represents proportional equality while the second is individual equality. The most radical form is the Marxist variant which equates wages with need and effort with ability. An adjustment of this (Marxist) concept of equality is found in the progressive tax system which levies a higher tax on "broad shoulders" compared to people in the lower income brackets, who also receive benefits from society for the satisfaction of their needs, such that a greater or lesser degree of equalisation, and hence social equality of individual persons, is achieved, in parallel to or dependent on political equality.

ANTHROPOLOGY AND POLITICS

In practical politics, the question is therefore how political equality and justice may be administered without violating economic justice (payment by just dessert). John Rawls' "justice as fairness" attempts to balance these two concepts of justice through a "procedural justice". A modern variation of the social contract ensures that "reason" sees its own advantage in a certain form of political "inequality", allowing justice of payment to make the strong rich, as long as this benefits the weakest groups in society. Rawls' social model, which inclines towards social democracy, corresponds to the Danish Social Democratic prime minister Viggo Kampmann's statement (in 1960): "Let us harness capitalism to the social waggon!" The issue is not to make everybody equally poor, as happens in socialist states, but to turn people's sense of payment for just dessert to increase total welfare, as long as an optimal redistribution of the growth in wealth is ensured politically. The tax debate of recent years shows an increasing understanding of the fact that the tax system is not a suitable regulator of social justice, as progressive taxation encourages tax creativity, thus neutralising progression and obstructing activities.

In consequence of this we see a considerable theoretical and practical movement for "deregulation" with some theorists, such as Jürgen Habermas (b. 1929), in the name of liberty and reason speaking in favour of participation, by which they understand grassroots democracy. Others argue in favour of "privatisation", i.e. of leaving as much as possible to private autonomy or market mechanisms. In the former case the essence is: I decide, you pay!, in the latter case: I decide, I pay! Habermas and his supporters are indebted to a belief going back to antiquity and the Enlightenment that the social nature of human beings will lead human reason to choose what is good, as in principle what is "good" may be achieved by a reasonable choice. The "privatisation model" is based on a view of man as a selfish creature: that we think first of ourselves, and that society must therefore set the limits of individual freedom. This view of human nature corresponds to Kant's distinction between knowledge and value judgements, and hence with the need of *normative* morality. If man were fundamentally a social being there would be no need for a normative morality, as morality is a surrogate for the instincts genetically governing the human ability of self-identification. As it is, our self-identification does not reach much further than to the closest family or the small family groups which formed the social framework around the hunter-gatherer cultures which shaped our genes. Everything belonging to the "large society" built by people by the force of their culture-creating reason and corresponding poverty of instincts must be learned and indoctrinated through *normative* morals and law (F.A. Hayek (1899-1992)).

There is much to indicate that the "concept of justice" is linked with our *anthropology*, and that we have a genetic predisposition to our spontaneous reaction against "injustice", although the content of the concept varies, and although there is no corresponding concept in Asian and African cultures. The fact that the concept has not been formulated in these cultures is not, however, the same as saying that it does not exist in reality.

There appears to be a universal human attitude behind the concept of "just payment and just retribution". Even in the most primitive societies, groups "trade" with each other through the exchange of goods. The goods are often left in fixed spots, and when enough values have been offered in return for the services offered, the "payment" is removed and the "agreement" concluded. Gift-giving rituals and rituals of exchange are common in most cultures and serve to strengthen ties within the group.

Revenge and retaliation also appear to be universal means of reaction in primitive cultures, later ritualised into a more or less developed system of composition. Religious sacrificial rituals also appear to be universal, based as they are on the idea that higher powers must be placated or softened with gifts, and that misfortune is punishment for "wrongdoings" which must be expiated.

The counterpart of the notion of justice must thus also be sought in anthropological factors. Human beings are social animals, in so far as the species would not be able to survive unless somebody takes care of the young for a very long period, and this requires extensive social organisation and some division of labour. It is therefore important that the individual persons should feel comfortable with a considerable level of *order* based on mutual trust and compliance with the rules. The appellation "just" applies to the person who is inclined to follow the law in this form.

Biological factors can also influence perceptions of justice, as indicated by psychological analyses of women and men's perception of "justice". While women appear to associate actual care for others with the concept, men appear to a greater degree to associate principles and abstract concerns with it (Source: Henrik Poulsen, Professor of Psychology, University of Aarhus).

"Fair", "not to make a distinction", "reliable", "trustworthy", "impartial", "upright", "objective", "altruistic", "incorruptible", are some of the synonyms emphasised as characteristic of the just ruler, the just judge, and the just father. "He shares out sun and wind in equal portions", says an old Danish proverb, implying that everybody gets the same amount of sun and wind on their fields. "Do your duty and demand your right", is another moral-political saying. "Give each man his due", says Ezekiel (33), and Solomon wants to make a Solomonic decision in the case of the child. *"Pax et justitia"*, *"justitia fundamentum regnorium"* is one variation of the motto of the Danish Renaissance King Christian IV, and it shows that peace and the fear of God are the ends for the building of society, justice its vital condition. But the highest law, *"summum ius, summa iniuria"*, is simultaneously also the highest injustice, as the law must be administered with fairness and equity, *"aequum et bonum"*, in good faith, *"Treu und Glauben"*, fairness and reason. Strict justice is Piso's justice. According to legend, the Roman general Piso sentenced a man to death for the murder of a friend and left him to a centurion, who, when the friend came back alive, sent the condemned man and the friend to the General. With the words: *"Fiat justitia, ruat coelum"*, justice must take its course, though the heavens fall down, Piso executed all three, the condemned man because he had been sentenced to death, the friend because he was the cause of the sentence, and the commander because he had disobeyed his order.

JUST WAR AND POSITIVE LAW

Justum bellum, or the just war, is a topical variation of justice. The notion goes back to Cicero, but it was only developed at the time of the late Roman Empire by St. Augustine, who wanted to reconcile the Christian principle which rejected killing and war with the right to wage war under certain circumstances capable of *justifying* the war. First and foremost, defensive warfare is just, but even a war of aggression may be justified by its end, such as the liberation of suppressed nations or national groups in order to secure their right of self-determination; in general, a war was only justified when its end goal was peace. *Pax et justitia* was the purpose of the states of princes in relation to the State of God. A "lawful" war must also follow a certain procedure, often a declaration of war. In United Nations procedure, adoption by the Security Council is an indispensable part.

The theory of just war is related to the natural law theory of the *right of reaction* against a tyrannical ruler and the modern theory of "civil disobedience". Another element in the debate has also been the theory of "positive discrimination", which argues the justice of discriminating in favour of weaker social groups. In the USA these include mainly black people and other ethnic groups, in Europe mainly women. It may be doubted whether legal and moral arguments are able to justify the waiving by authorities of the general rule that a formal principle of equality must apply in public administration.

To sum up, originally the word "just" meant "in accordance with the law". This meaning, which is natural for all primitive societies, where the law is seen as *divine custom*, also accords with the Old Testament, Ancient Greek, and Medieval European meaning of the word. It is, however, brought into doubt when and as the law is changed to become a positive *instrument of social control*.

With this change in the concept of law, a conflict may arise between positive law and natural law, that is to say the moral law.

In Greek culture, the schism arose when the positive and conventional Sophist concept of law was confronted with the Socratic and post-Socratic ethical and anthropological criticism. In Jewish culture, justice changes with Christ's criticism of the law and later with the Church dogma on justification and absolution through the atonement of Christ.

In European culture the concept of justice changes with the recognition of a secular law-making competence around the mid-1200s and with the moral censure which follows upon Catholic moral philosophy and later rationalist natural law.

It is clear that the concept of justice, especially in political theory and practice, readily turns into the "value judgements of the intending purchaser", as justice is easily identified with the interests of the speaker. In this light it is understandable that logical empiricism and the realist theory of law rejected the concept as meaningless. Nevertheless, the content and structure of the concept do deserve discussion.

The fact is that the concept of justice is not applied indiscriminately. From ancient times it has had a certain structure, although its content has changed. References to "equality" in one or another sense have always proved to be an essential element in the concept when subjected to logical analysis. Although equality means different things and refers different contexts to different criteria, it is important to maintain that an assessment of equality is a fixed component of the concept. The "isonomic" common element in law and justice, "equality before the law", is also emphasised by Pericles and Demosthenes, who developed the theory of democracy, while the "proportionate" or corrective element was emphasised by more conservative thinkers such as Aristotle. Equality is judged differently in different contexts, but the crucial judgement is arguably the one which stresses what is *regular* in contrast to what is *arbitrary*. People require a state of order, both in society and in their minds.

THE LAW OF REACTION

Experiences from the legal political debate of recent generations on the law of reaction have shown that rational resolutions to problems under criminal or compensation law have failed, for the reason, it seems, that a need exists for retaining the concept of *responsibility* as justification for retribution against crimes and other harmful acts under both criminal law and compensation law.

In the area of criminal law, the popular theory of special prevention failed dismally during the first half of this century. Its ideology was the popular belief, also held by Marxist theory, that crime is caused by societal or individual defects of a kind which led individual persons into crime. To change society or treat the criminal was therefore the goal which would make crime disappear gradually.

Various kinds of institutions for treatment were established: psychiatric wards, safe custody of psychopaths, houses of correction, youth prisons, etc., all for the purpose of improving the criminal rather than punishing him. Gradually, it was found that the treatment had no significant effect compared with normal imprisonment; relapse rates remained the same. As offenders undergoing treatment also saw their placing as a punishment, the indefinite nature of the detention was felt to be unjust.

The system was criticised both by the left and the right, as both wings wanted *responsibility* reintroduced as reason and criterion for the judgement. The Norwegian criminologist Nils Christie (b. 1928) spoke directly of "theft of responsibility", and the Danish Alf Ross argued in a book for the reintroduction of neo-Classical criminal law based on guilt, responsibility and imprisonment in the absence of better measures, although it was clear that punishment had no positive effect, and although there was no connection between the severity of the punishment and relapse into crime.

Within compensation law, a legal-political movement arose in the thirties, both in the USA and Scandinavia, with the aim of replacing compensation law with insurance arrangements, especially in cases of personal injury. These insurances were intended to cover losses and to release tortfeasors from responsibility, except in cases of wilful harm or gross negligence. Much progress was achieved towards compensating most work accidents with suitable fixed rate compensations through the development of work, accident and social insurances. The aim was to prevent compensation claims against tortfeasors, but we have seen that public and political requirements have led to both special legislation and ordinary legislation in supplement of these arrangements, with compensation claims under private law based on *responsibility*.

Following a couple of generations' battle for "impartial" solutions to major social problems, we are forced to resign ourselves to failure and realise that people's sense of responsibility and justice appear to be ineradicable. Nobody can avoid responsibility although the damage is compensated, and it must be possible to claim damages from somebody when you've been injured. Somebody must be made responsible!

JUSTICE IN LITERATURE

In literature, we find illustrations of the four forms of justice discussed here. The concept of just payment is illustrated in a story I believe to be by Halldor Laxness; the isonomic justice in a scene from Alexander Dumas' *The Count of Monte Christo*; the concept of justice as equity in Shakespeare's *Merchant of Venice*; and natural law justice in Sophocles' tragedy *Antigone*.

The first of these stories, which I believe to have read in Laxness' *Frie Mænd*, although the author himself does not recall the story, provides an example of the principle of contractual justice under substantive law, that if a person receives a good or a bad thing, an obligation is created requiring either repayment or compensation. The rule is called quasi contract or equity. But we know from anthropology that the principle is general in nature, and as noted, we find it illustrated in the following story, which despite my conviction cannot be ascribed to Laxness with any certainty.

An elderly couple is spending an Arctic night hungry and cold in their dirt hut. When a notorious witch passes, the desperate man invites her in, and as she refuses the invitation, he grabs her, dragging her inside. She is offered a meagre meal, but refuses this too, so the desperate couple force feed her, declaring triumphantly that she is now obliged to assist them in their trouble. Nothing daunted, however, the witch goes outside and, leaving the disappointed couple with a triumphant laugh, she vomits, thus releasing herself of the obligation.

In one chapter, Dumas tells the story of how the Count and his companion happen to witness an execution. Two condemned men allow themselves to be led meekly to the scaffold, when one of them is pardoned, upon which the other man launches into desperate resistance as he will not be killed if the other is pardoned.

Just as the first story reflects a primitive mentality's making of law through objective actions or formulae, the third story, Shakespeare's *Merchant*, refers to a primitive legal institution, personal liability, according to which a debtor was liable for his debt with his person, which meant that his creditor had the right to kill him, turn him into a slave, or, as here, cut a pound of flesh from him. The strict law is clear, and the creditor is supported in his right, but the humane judge turns the strictness of the law against the creditor himself with the proviso: "But not one drop of blood". By application of this trick, the judge humanises the strict law by fixing a condition which cannot be fulfilled, and which thus appears as an equitable solution.

In the drama of Sophocles, we also see how the strict law pervading the tragedies of the elder Aischylos is penetrated by a natural law concept. Against the King's orders, Antigone buries her dead brother, and when accused of having defied positive law, she defends herself against her accusers by claiming the superordinate eternal unwritten divine law which demands that relatives bury their dead. Aristotle was later to use this scene in his *Rhetoric* as illustration of his natural l..w theory.

Thus, one cannot justify "justice" with reference to a pre-existing moral obligation to act justly towards other human beings or God, as any such reference *presupposes* the existence of an obligation. Morality presupposes the concept of "duty", as obligation starts where inclination stops. This is why a "realist" or "naturalist" theory of law is impossible, because it presupposes that the law is legal behaviour or a "sense of duty", this being a condition for predicting the behaviour. According to such theories, the psychopath is thus not obligated, feeling as he does neither any concrete duty to follow a given rule limiting his freedom of action, or in general any duty to respect the rules of law.

JUSTICE AND DUTY

The special thing about "duty" as a normative concept is exactly that it is possible to speak of a legal or moral "duty", although the person in question has no desire to act in accordance with the "duty".

The anarchist recognises no duty to follow a rule which he does not want to follow, and by this stand he attacks the very basis of any organised society — the benefits of which the anarchist is often quite ready to enjoy — as willingness to accept restrictions in individual freedom presupposes mutuality. This is what we have called isonomic justice. The anarchist's or psychopath's attitude thus cannot pass the universality argument, as it cannot form the rule by which a society is structured unless its individual members are recognised as fundamentally social beings, which political and criminological experience tells us people are not, at least not in relation to our "big societies" established by reason. Whether we would be social beings in the "natural state", the "small society" corresponding to our genes, is doubtful even at the hypothetical level. A condition of the human ability to create culture is our extreme poverty of instincts, and this means that we cannot be certain that human beings would act "in a social manner" in the natural state, as do other animals who are protected by their very strong instincts against tendencies which could destroy the species. In contrast to other animal species, people are, for example, capable of killing other members of their own species. Claims of organised "warfare" or deathly feuds among groups of chimpanzees have not been convincingly documented.

One cannot automatically take the customs of existing primitive cultures as one's basis. For one thing, our ancestors must have been different from the people in the existing static cultures, or they would not have started a dynamic cultural development. Also, "customs" are not completely static, but are subject to constant change, and finally even the most primitive cultures have believed that their customs had a magic/ritual divine and hence "binding" nature.

The same non-empirical (naturalist) explanation of morality is found in E. Hammershaimb (1904-94), who seeks the reason for the movement from the Old Testament collective ethics to the New Testament subjective ethics precisely in the cultural changes in society. With the collapse of the nomadic family structure following the immigration into the coastal cities of the Philistines and of the "barter justice" associated with the division of work, the old and the young lost their social value, which had previously been high, and had to be protected by a new morality. In a dynamic society, the experience of old people is of less value, and the value of children as future providers diminishes with the chance of saving an "unlimited" fortune in money. Therefore, Hammershaimb says, because there is no longer a direct interest, it becomes necessary to establish an abstract "duty" if society is to function.

The same line of thought is expressed in the work of the brothers Westermark on the basis and development of moral values from the same anthropological and cultural angle. Their thesis is that as the human genetically based social sense of identification is limited to the closest family, we must "learn" through ethical principles to "love" larger and larger groups of people in step with the integration of ever increasing social groups into the larger society.

Moral and legal norms could well be called surrogates for the instincts which keep other animal species in a state of social balance. On the one hand this is the explanation of the ever increasing identification process with the Christian radical dogma at one extreme, and on the other hand it is a *memento* to the effect that there are limits to how quickly and how effectively multicultural integration can take place. There is no art in loving the beautiful, the rich and the good. But *morality* must ask that we also love the ugly, the poor and the wicked, an act which will yield us no direct advantage, for it is old knowledge that mutual benefit is a social basis of lasting friendship. This was the moral of Carl Ewald's fable of the lobster and the sea anemone living in symbiosis. When the lobster had to change its shell, it asked cautiously what guarantee it would have that the sea anemone would not be tempted to feast on the lobster's exposed body during the change. None!, answered the sea anemone, but what guarantees do I have that you will take me along on your new shell? None!, was the answer. But the story ends happily, of course to the satisfaction of both parties. Distributive justice comes into conflict with corrective justice when society develops.

The crucial problem is that the immediate benefit must be exchanged for future greater benefit, and as the common advantage of this arrangement is not immediately clear to everybody at all times, the collective consciousness will require support by an abstract moral principle. The argument underlying the new welfare theory is the same as that which in "prisoner's dilemma" illustrates the importance of social trust, a trust which partly prevents individual persons from injuring the circumstances of other persons in order to secure maximum advantage for themselves, and partly forces them to limit their own advantage.

The psychopath only engages in single transactions, as it is vital for the established tradesman to appear as an "ethical" and "fair" trader whose promises may be believed, a person worthy of general trust. There exists, and must perforce exist, a close link between reason and morality and law, but where reason no longer suffices, morality and law must fulfil their duty.

SYMMETRY AND JUSTICE

"It's unfair, he didn't deserve that!" This is an expression which reveals the symmetrical structure of the concept of justice, the balance between crime and punishment, between service and payment, between deed and just desserts.

Primitive perceptions of justice are objective. They see the process of justice in terms of an imbalancing event releasing a harmonising effect. The right and duty of revenge is a matter for the group and is released by a harmful fact inflicted on a member of the group, and it may retaliate on any member of the offending group. *Talion* represents a limitation on the right of revenge to involve no more than a similar offence. Rather than being the gruesome punishment which later generations have seen in it, *talion* represent a civilising step.

As we see in Greek and Norse mythology, retribution involves an element of fate. The Moerae and the Norns spin, measure up and cut the human thread of life as given by one's lot in life. Justice only enters the life of individual people when this divine meting out has taken place, as they are thereafter entitled to benefits according to their lot. To each his due!

It is no accident that the Danish word for "lot" means both fate and weight, as prior to coinage, all valuation was normally done by weight. *Mene, mene tekel* probably contains a reference to *minas* and *shekels*, which were Babylonian units of weight used as a measure of value similar to the British "one weight in gold". In its formulae and rituals, early Roman law retained elements of the time when business took place at the marketplace with weighing on scales (*per aes et libram*).

In all Middle Eastern cultures from ancient Egypt to Babylon, the scales were also the symbol of the divine weighing of the individual human life. Baat weighs the hearts of dead people against a feather. If it is too light, it is left to the monster of death. Similar notions spread to the eastern Semites in Babylon and may later have influenced Jewish culture, although it could also be a case of shared Semite myths. The same applies to the secular *casuist* laws and their systems of composition which may be found as far back as in Hittite and Babylonian laws of the second millennium BC, and are taken over by the old Mosaic laws in addition to the *categorical* laws with their nature of divine command: thou shalt, thou shalt not, etc. As we saw, these latter laws reflect the fundamental conditions under which the society was able to function dressed up as religious sanctions promising salvation or damnation.

Despite all other differences, the later Christian formulation is constructed according to the same symmetric rhetorical model, although the reaction has become the opposite. Revenge is the Lord's (and Caesar's); the injured must turn the other cheek. It is no longer the case that justification is achieved through individual deeds, but only through the suffering and death of Christ. Original sin is atoned through proxy, just as Isaac was replaced by the scapegoat in Abraham's sacrifice. Yet the structure has been retained with its focus on sin and atonement, guilt and justification. The notion of a future day of judgement is also retained where the just shall be separated from the damned. This *ethical* dualism of late Jewish-Christian nature is of doubtful origin but related to the Persian Zoroastrian religion.

One thing that is known, however, is the fact that in the 6th and 7th century BC, Persian dualism began to influence Greek thinking, especially in the Pythagorean numerical symmetry, which was later taken over by Aristotle in his theory of corrective justice. At the same time, the scales continued to represent justice, although the cosmological displacement, which meant that at the time of the autumnal equinox, the axis of the earth had moved from the sign of the scales into that of the virgin, led the Greeks to place the scales in the hand of the virgin. Later, the virgin Dice with the sword became the Roman *Lady Justitia*, who later again, during the Baroque period, had her eyes covered, not to indicate the blindness of the law, but its impartiality.

During the European Middle Ages, the combination of casuist law with the system of composition and just payment was reformulated by Christian ethics into a dogma of guilt and subjective evidence, by which punishment was tied to intention or negligence and contractual obligation to moral will, according to which no more could be demanded than just payment, *justum pretium*. The cultural latitude required for the full introduction of subjective evidence into secular law took some time to evolve. As late as the 1200s, in his Latin paraphrase of the regional law, *Skånske Lov*, the Danish archbishop and jurist Anders Sunesen (1165-1228) felt obliged to excuse the secular objective law with reference to the "rational" argument that the pain is the same whether it be inflicted with or without ill will. It was not until the 1700s that *culpa* fully penetrated European compensation law under influence from rationalist natural law theory. Under its influence, Catholic moral philosophy and theory of legislation developed during the 1600s and 1700s into a general subjective and moral theory of will and contract based on the proposition that *moral* will required a just balance: "You shouldn't take more in than you have paid out!", or *quid pro quo*.

The theory of "just payment" goes back to the ancient Greek theory of value as a tangible quality in things. This theory received its death blow with the British empiricist philosophy, when Hume's criticism of natural law and Adam Smith's theory of market economics destroyed every belief that value was any other than notions of value in the operator valuing the market, a value which he *invests* in the object. One must seek other means of ensuring a just balance in matters concerning the law. The utilitarian theory imposes a moral duty on society to protect the weak against exploitation, while others have pointed to an "invisible hand" (Adam Smith) or free competition. Experience has shown that none of these mechanisms will ensure "justice" unaided. The invisible hand was probably based on the faith of natural law in the social nature of human beings, while market economics put its faith in everybody's equal strategic position in the market, but since the industrial revolution, which divided people into producers and consumers, this has no longer been the reality. Legislation attempts to secure "justice" through rules of nullity, rules which constitute in part an extension of the old rules of equity: force, fraud, delusion, exploitation, and in part new general clauses aimed at safeguarding individual persons against "*unreasonable*" contractual terms, especially the standards terms of business people.

JUSTICE AS PROCESS

"That wasn't fair!" is a term referring to the procedural variant of justice. For justice to be done, it must be seen to be done. It is of little use being in the right if right is not being done.

In ancient times, "gods" were means of reaching a just decision. A duel was arranged according to certain rituals, and it was then left to God to decide who was right. Other divine judgements such as ordeal by fire or water etc. similarly constituted methods used in primitive times to reach a legal decision on a politically or objectively difficult matter. In most parts of Europe, gods were later replaced by oaths given by the family of the accused. They guaranteed that the accused was an honest person, but not that there was any evidence in favour of his case. An oath is thus not proof of cause, but an objective assurance and guarantee on behalf of the accused supported by faith.

Canon law characterised by its individualist theory takes its basis in the act and thus in the evidence of what actually took place, in the first instance through witnesses, but if possible also through documentation and other written material. The object of the procedure is *truth* rather than the *certainty* associated with a sacred oath. The justice emerging from the two procedures is also different. This is illustrated by the Norwegian author Johan Falkberget in his books on life in the ironworks at Røros at the time of the Renaissance king Christian IV, where we witness a historic clash of the two procedures. An oath is sworn that a certain woman has killed her newborn baby, but a later professional examination by a doctor shows the woman to be a virgin. The population is divided over the two kinds of justice, the certainty provided by the old system based on oaths and the truth provided by the new system of proof.

The human rights procedural system is based primarily on the principle: *audiatur et altera pars*. Everybody knows as well as does any armchair politician that the last honourable speaker always appears to be right. In English speaking countries, a "fair trial" will often be associated with the decision of "twelve good men" in the form of a jury, while the function of the judge often resembles that of an umpire, who must ensure that the rules of the game are being kept, but otherwise merely draws the legal consequences of the decisions made by the jury. On the European continent, where a jury is an exception, the judge holds considerable power to assess evidence, and *freedom to consider evidence* is an important principle of law compared to the "right to bring proof" of primitive societies, where fixed rules of priority limit the discretionary powers of the judge.

An important principle in the administration of justice is the *independence* of the judge *vis á vis* public authorities and his *lack of competence* where personal interest is involved. *Lady Justitia*'s eyes are covered to emphasise that justice is impersonal. This is an ideal which has not always proved true, certainly not in the hierarchical and class-riven societies of the past. In totalitarian societies the judge is a tool of the political system, as was the case in the Third Reich and in communist states. Independent courts were an absolute requirement in John Locke's and Montesquieu's visions of a democratic system based on individual freedom and its consequent "human rights". Power corrupts, so it is essential to divide the legislative, executive and judicial powers of government.

Judge Lynch is the strict but just judge who sentences his own son to death for murder, despite his wife's begging for mercy. This morbid myth of impersonal justice is countered by general rules of competence to act, aimed at safeguarding the parties against being given a judge who cannot make an "impartial" decision for reasons of personal interest or personal association with one of the parties. "There must be no doubt of the virtue of Caesar's wife", as the emperor said when divorcing his wife, not because he thought her guilty of sacrilege, but because she had brought herself into a situation where her virtue could be doubted.

Socrates submitted to an "unjust" sentence and emptied the cup of poison because of an ancient Greek respect for the law, just as the Saxons submitted to the divine judgement in the duel between Uffe and the Saxon prince in the story told by Saxo Grammaticus. In similar manner people have submitted to proof by oath and the communist leaders to party decisions in the infamous Moscow proceedings and later proceedings in Eastern Europe. As loyal party member, one played the role assigned to one by the party script, as this was what the shared ideology prescribed.

It is clear that a different kind of justice will result from the different types of proceedings, but the concept of "fair trial" is undoubtedly a concept with a structure tied to the commonly accepted legal and procedural system. In our minds, the concept is inseparably tied to the ideology of individualism and constitutional government, which distances itself from older and younger theories on the superior value of reasons of state and social utility. The individual member of society has a legal space which cannot be violated by administration or legislation, but merely delimited by a judicial authority in a "fair trial".

Knud Illum's inaugural speech of 1951 as vice-chancellor was called "False weights in *Lady Justitia*'s scales", and was based on the thesis that in order to be "just", the legal decision must not only be made by a judge in accordance with the procedural principles discussed here, but would also require convincing grounds. "False weights" are arguments which are either superfluous or self-contradictory, or have no authority in "recognised" sources of law. The judge may not use "invalid arguments" and believe that by using more invalid arguments still, he will arrive at a valid argument. Zero + zero will never equal one. Neither may the judge "invent" rules which do not exist in order to use them as grounds for a decision wanted for other reasons.

These warnings should appear superfluous, but Illum showed in his speech that they are not. The most dangerous point, after all, is not that judges are free to consider evidence and free in their ranking of acknowledged legal source materials. There are of course good judges and bad judges, just as there are good tradesmen and bad tradesmen or doctors. The greatest danger does, however, lie in the language qualification of the facts presented for evaluation. Our language is a tool for our purposes and cannot be objective, so it is misleading and dangerous for a theory to speak of the "objective content of rules" etc. There is of course an "intersubjective" content in language as it could not otherwise fulfil its function as a means of communication. Like language, rules of law are "teleological", as their purpose is to regulate social behaviour, and the rules must therefore be "interpreted" in accordance with their purpose and effect, that is to say, interpreted in teleological and pragmatic terms. But to safeguard the rule of law, and this is an essential element in our understanding of justice as the protection of individual persons, the interpretation of law must proceed on the basis of "ordinary" language use. This is the interpretation which the addressee is "authorised" to apply to his actions, the only starting point, unless the demand for the publication of laws is to become an illusion. In cases of doubt, preliminaries and motives may be brought in to contribute to the interpretation, but in cases where a clear discrepancy will disadvantage individual citizens, the rule of law must demand an interpretation based in the "wording". Social utility or political intentions cannot, in a constitutional society, be given preference. In the construction of the welfare state which was seen as the "friend" and "benefactor" of the population, the courts went far in the direction of accepting "blanket laws" and the motives given with regard to the intention of the legislators and administrative practices. More recently, with the "high tax society" and the "corporate state", where power is delegated to interest groups and the consensus reached by interest groups on councils and boards, the state has become an "enemy", and it has again become the task of the courts to prune the state in its relationship with the individual citizen. In accordance with this trend we see an increasing tendency towards emphasis on the rule of law and the wording of the law at the cost of motives and administrative practice which cannot be changed without warning. Especially tax law has seen a development in this direction, but other sub-systems of administrative law must submit to correction on the grounds of equality, "abuse of power", "point of fact" and "suitability". References to "fairness" and other primary value judgements are no longer considered out of bounds, even without explicit legal authority.

COMPETENCE TO ACT

In the context of an analysis of a "fair trial" and its inherent condition of "equal" and "impartial" treatment, it is worth remembering the old rule according to which everybody has the right to be judged by his equals.

In the old hierarchical society, the clergy were judged by ecclesiastical courts, noblemen by their peers, military men by military courts and students by the university senate. In Denmark, peasants had to resort to district courts, but were probably not likely to receive much "impartiality" in complaints against their lords, who often held the right to appoint the district judge. Public judgements in private law reports do, however, show that peasants were able to win a case against a lord, but it was probably the exception rather than the rule.

Under procedural law, special rules have been fixed governing the competence to act in cases of conflicting interests. Under these rules, the judge must vacate his seat if one of the parties is a relation, or if he has other strong interests in the case. In the so-called "Hauschildt Case", the Human Rights Commission decided that a judge who has repeatedly committed an accused to trial in consequence of a charge on "special grounds" cannot preside at the trial, as his impartiality relative to his own former dispositions may be brought into doubt, and Danish procedural law has been changed accordingly.

In public administration it has become more difficult to uphold the requirement of "competence to act" as a condition of validity, as the normal situation at the present time may be said to be one where interest groups fill the political assemblies in city councils, regional councils and parliament. Parliament legislates on the basis of interests, as laws may be said to be the jousting ground for conflicting interests. The worrying element is the fact that legislation only mediates current interests, without weighing them against the general interests of the public at large.

This is precisely the Achilles heel of democracy, the fact that demands on the public sector are formulated by strong interests, as public expenses are always private income, while the population as a whole is only poorly represented. In local and regional administrations the problem is more urgent, as concrete decisions are made here on matters directly affecting the decision makers or their support groups. This is the reason why it used to be unthinkable for a teacher as member of the city council to take part in the discussion of matters affecting schools. But in his 1987 thesis, Steen Rønsholdt shows how this has changed so that only a *concrete* interest can lead to invalidity, while in practical terms a rule of nullity in cases involving a general conflict of interests cannot be upheld without making municipal government impossible, as more than half of the population is now employed by or dependent on public funds.

The situation is especially difficult in appeals. Regional politicians who are employees in the primary municipality are empowered to handle complaints from the sector in which they themselves are employed. Practice has restricted conflict of interest to cover only people who have taken an active part in the handling of the case, and not people who are merely employed in the department in question.

In university administration, employee democracy has led to a further exacerbation of the situation in that the decision makers in governing bodies are not only representatives of interest groups, but in the case of teachers, they are the decisive element in the decision-making process: they are also both colleagues and competitors. The time is long past when, in a case of professional evaluation, one might say "NN is such a staunch enemy of mine that I will always be able to trust him to treat me fairly". The old system of civil service was based on an ethos of professional quality and professional responsibility which served to prevent at least the most glaring instances of mixing professional and other (irrelevant) considerations.

THE MERITS OF A CASE: LAW AND POLITICS

In order to accept a decision as just, it must thus not only correspond to the substance of certain norms, but the procedure must also follow certain rules, and a distinction must be made between objective and non-objective considerations. A legal decision must be independent of the parties' economic, social and political status, their sex and race, and this is the aim of rules governing competence to act and procedure as well as the demand for objective argumentation. "Positive discrimination" just as much as "negative discrimination" must be held to be in conflict with formal justice. It would be dangerous to pursue "material justice", equal pay for women, equal work for all ages, races etc. through discriminatory rules which can lead to a distortion of mentality. This is also the case when it is claimed in the environmental debate that the "environment must be given a chance", such that an expense is justified unless it can be proved that it is superfluous. To abandon the principles of law in the service of the "good" is the first step on the road towards a totalitarian society.

Experience has also shown that it is dangerous to pursue social objectives through taxation, as the progressive scale used for this purpose works partly as an incentive to creative tax schemes and partly to "black work", and partly becomes self-contradictory when average incomes end by paying an expensive price for their own welfare. This is apart from the fact that a "prohibitive" income tax presents an obstacle to economic activity. The taxation system should be a public financing system organised for optimum effectiveness for this purpose, while social objectives should be resolved through social policies.

Like the Christiania Case, the "Tamil Affair" (minister accused of administering refugee laws *contra legem*, but according to what he believed was the majority view in parliament) shows how dangerous to justice it is when the political system gives up in the face of its own incompetence and decides instead to turn problems into law by leaving them to a court, examination by a magistrate, or to a tribunal of inquiry.

On the one hand, the independence and prestige of judges and the law are compromised by engagement in a political fight. On the other hand, the authority of the law is misused to gloss or denigrate certain political interests or acts which are thus made "unlawful" or "unjust".

By claiming various constitutional guarantees, the critical ideology of the 1960s and 70s had some luck in gaining political advantages by using the courts as a tool of social change. Especially in the USA and Germany, which are federal states with only one common constitution and thus a greater degree of political competence vested in the courts, many party reforms were achieved through judgements. Racial integration for one was introduced in this manner, but the movement became stuck when the courts refused to become involved in the placing of nuclear power plants. In Denmark, the supreme court refused to decide whether "Christiania" was a "social experiment". This is the limit of the competence of the courts, because they are not elected with a political mandate.

The law can thus be used both by and against political rulers. Examples include the deployment of legal weapons against the labour movement and the "right to strike" in earlier periods (T. Wanscher), and in more recent times the union movement has used "physical blockades" and other "legal" means for more far-reaching political gains.

These cases are all instances of "false weights in *Lady Justitia*'s scales", as the law is not used as the reason for the activities, but as their pretext. They are therefore not instances of "impartial" and "fair" trials, and are therefore "unjust".

REASONABLE AND JUST

The uncertain and changing use of language seen in the use of the word "reasonable" reveals a corresponding uncertainty in the theoretical debate. The general language use is a distillate of a former avant garde discussion in the same way as the habits of the aristocracy gradually sink into petty bourgeois copying. It is a well-known fact that the bourgeoisie's fashions of dress and furnishings and its ideal culture at the turn of the century, in the 20s and 30s became the pattern of the petty bourgeois social democrats with no aspirations for a distinct "proletarian culture".

Within jurisprudence, Scandinavian realism, which was closely related to the social democratic theory of welfare and its functional view of the concept of law, did, however, in principle distance itself from bourgeois idealism and the traditional concept of duty. Rules of law were seen as "free-standing imperatives" or tools of the "state's monopolised apparatus of force". The sense of right and duty was not the cause but the consequence of "positive law". The purpose of psychology, education and the law was to adapt the individual to society and not the other way around, as individuals cannot have "rights" which come into conflict with the state's superior interests in increasing "social utility". Jurisprudence becomes socio-psychology or legal politics.

At any rate, value judgements and statements involving evaluation cease to have meaning, as they do not describe qualities in things, but the valuer's feelings, or because they lack "semantic reference", as there is no measurable counterpart to the semantic claim in the external world. Among the proponents of this view, Alf Ross was the most consistent in his acceptance of logical empiricism, which demanded on the one hand empirical measuring of data also for sociological descriptions, and on the other presupposed that objective descriptions are possible.

As in principle the latter is an impossibility according to the anthropological-hermeneutic perception of the function of language, the former become meaningless. It is an unrealistic and unsuitable theory, especially with regard to jurisprudence, for similarly to the arts and theology, jurisprudence is primarily a science of interpretation. Legal rules require interpretation just as art and religious texts do, and similarly to theological texts they must be interpreted as authoritative texts, i.e. on the assumption that the authority establishes a binding meaning. With regard to the rules of law, however, the interpretation must also adopt a teleological, or rational, and a pragmatic, or functional, angle. And finally in the interest of the rule of law, consideration must be given to the understanding which the addressees are "authorised" to apply.

In any case, a natural corollary of the realist school of thought was its rejection with scorn and derision of every reference to "fairness" and "justice", a scorn which presumably reflected the ideological-political content of the apparently neutral "theory of science". This presumption is supported by the subsequent "revolution" which in many places, but especially in China, took its starting point in a debate on the "correct" theory of science. Marxist theory was used extensively as a political means, and for some years not without success, as taught by their experiences of the inter-war years, post-war western countries had deliberately eliminated "ideologies". Logical empiricism was itself an expression of this effort.

The functionalist-pragmatic face of western democracies made them defenceless against new ideological attacks which pointed them out as reactionary and suppressive. Its lack of philosophical training, coupled with a constitutional Protestant "sense of guilt" of own riches, laid the "established society" wide open to the "critical science", the purpose of which was "not to interpret, but to change reality".

The established elite had been taught that an act could not be "right", "fair" or "just". It could, however, be "correct" and "practicable". This meant they were already half beaten by any attacker who knew the "truth" and therefore knew what was "right" and "just" by force of his alliance with both the purpose of development as well as the necessary and final revelation of "truth".

In the meantime, the scientific consensus had sunk into general language, where it had now become a matter of course that you "cannot argue about matters of taste", and where language use as a whole changes from "right" to "correct" and from "fair" to "practicable". The latter formulation is of course meaningless, as nothing can be practicable without having a purpose. The case was simply that the ghost had moved house and that intuitive (prohibited) value judgements had come to be made under cover of objective terms.

It is a curious feature that the word "practicable" in Danish came to be used in a wrong sense, replacing the term "fair", while in later usage the term "fair" has returned, but now also in a wrong meaning, its original and right meaning having been lost. In current daily language the term is now used in a quantitative sense, as in "fairly bad", "fairly large" etc. Its "right" meaning has not, however, been reestablished. Daily language use has thus turned the original meanings of the words upside down, so that "practicable" continues to be used in a qualitative sense for expressing a primary value judgement rather than an assessment of purpose/means, while "fair" is used in a quantitative sense in expressions of comparative value.

These examples of "wrong" language use are not just trivial expressions of "ordinary language change" which cannot be considered more or less "correct" or "right". If language is held to be a complementary component of our consciousness, this is no trivial or conventional shift in language, but a change of the structure of our minds which can have far-reaching consequences in our relationship with and description or handling of the external world.

If this theoretical debate is underpinned by a political debate, it is not a trivial matter whether we recognise or fail to recognise the meaning of terms such as "fair" and "just". If it is true that there is a need and a growing trend among judicial decision makers for using such primary value judgements as authoritative or normative elements in legal argumentation, we must recognise this need and formulate it in the "right" use of language.

JUSTICE AND NATURAL LAW

To refer to justice is not the same as to refer to natural law, although both concepts refer to moral demands of the law. Firstly, justice is a broader ethical concept, while natural law is a narrower legal or political concept, not based in Aristotle's ethics but in his politics. To Aristotle, natural law is identical with that which rational human nature, *zoon politicon*, will choose as the best form of government, and to him this was the Greek *polis*.

Aristotle's natural science or anthropological natural law concept had its social roots in the political development inspired by Plato's criticism in his story of Socrates of democratic Athens' unethical treatment of its allies and admirals during the Peloponnesian War against Sparta.

The criticism was directed not least against the Athenian practice of government, which meant that the people's assembly was in principle both a legislative and a judicial body, although a number, up to 100, were selected to handle special criminal cases. It goes without saying that any such political system will promote rhetoric rather than ethics or legal rule-oriented debate. We know the phenomenon from American jury cases, where the rhetorical *ad hominem* argumentation, which focuses on the person and not the case, marches triumphant.

Secondly, the absence of a distinction between general laws and actual judicial decisions meant that the decisions became emotional and unpredictable as well as subject to rapid change. The result is arbitrariness and "injustice", Plato claims, referring to the admirals who were executed, not formally because they had lost an important sea battle, but because they had failed to fulfil their religious duty of salvaging the bodies of the dead. Plato is even more contemptuous of the sentence given his old teacher Socrates, who was condemned to death for corrupting young people and mocking the gods. Plato believes that in both cases the "law" was used for "political" purposes, the violation of religious duties being merely a pretext, but an effective pretext to use in an inflamed popular assembly.

Although Aristotle cannot follow Plato in the latter's unsuccessful attempt at basing a social order on the sovereign reason of the "philosopher", he does support Plato's demand for "justice" in the form of general laws which set general rules for social life in the form of a society regulated less by functional laws than by a "natural" organisation. In contrast to Plato, who saw a kind of enlightened despotism as the best form of government, Aristotle was in favour of a democratic form of government, arguing that there is a better chance for all interests to be heard when everybody is entitled to take part in government, and in this way the "rational common will" may be realised.

He did, however, hold that democracy with no rules was a vulgar democracy equally as dangerous as despotism, as in a direct democracy, the demagogue is as dangerous as the flatterers of the despot!

As we know, the ancient Greek form of government and state was aristocratic with a customary law given by the gods. In the 500s BC, the Sophists turned this order upside down by claiming that just as people were not created by the gods, but gods by the people, thus the law is not made by the gods but by people themselves who by their free will have entered into a social contract, which is the authority of law. It follows that the law is *positive* or conventional, although it has its roots in a (fictive) social contract.

Aristotle accepted the notion of a social contract as basis of a democracy, but found as we saw that human nature and reason require the law to be expressed in rules according to justice. Aristotle's concept of equality did not, however, extend beyond people of equal rank. He did not object to slavery or discrimination against women. Underpinning his notion of distributive justice was the concept of *isonomy* or the belief that like cases should be treated alike. This was not a radical concept of equality, but an aristocratic concept of payment according to value and just dessert: *"suum (cuique tribuitur)"*.

It was the Hellenistic and Stoic belief that human beings are equal as individuals by the strength of their participation in divine reason combined with Christian individualism which later gave rise to the notion of human equality in the sense that people must be treated equally regardless of rank, class or nationality. It has been called a stroke of luck that Greece and Palestine were parts of the Roman empire at the same time, thus allowing Hellenism as well as Judaism and Christianity to spread and mix with ancient Roman concepts such as *jus* and *justitia, aequum et bonum* and to become common property through that peregrine praetor who extended (common) Roman law to include all nationalities in the empire.

The later Church concept of government as two swords reflects the crumbling Roman empire's need of power and law; and until the height of the Medieval period, natural law was seen as identical with the inscrutable will of the Lord, for people were sinful and must be chastised by God. In fact, St. Augustine held that law is the result of the fall from grace. The Church accepted this view, and it is found as late as in Anders Sunesen's *Hexaemeron* from the thirteenth century.

With Thomas Aquinas in the mid-1200s, the Aristotelian dogma of natural law was revived, based in man's social nature, *zoon politicon*, and in reason, which enables human beings to create a positive law by formulating the content of the natural law principles. While St. Augustine distinguished between divine and secular law and did not recognise any "law of reaction" if the emperor exceeded his powers, Thomas Aquinas did recognise a "right of reaction" if the positive law conflicted with divine law, but not if it only conflicted with natural law, although in that case it would be "invalid". With this, the investiture contest, i.e. the fight between the pope and the emperor about the right to appoint bishops, was over.

In subsequent centuries, a more extensive theory of human legislative competence (Marsilius) and of sovereignty (Bodin) was developed, but it was not until the thinkers of the seventeenth century, Grotius in Holland and Hobbes in England, that a radical argument in support of human legislative powers was developed, based on the ancient Greek notion of a social contract. While Grotius continued the Catholic ethical dogma of man as a social and rational being who takes independent initiative to organise himself legally, Hobbes reduced the social contract to a mere agreement to leave sovereignty to the prince.

While Grotius, based on his positive experiences and optimistic faith in human nature, laid the foundation of a later democratic social theory, Hobbes, in the hope of law and order and in the face of the threat of civil war, argued for enlightened despotism, and became the inspiration behind the Danish despotic constitution of 1661.

During the 1500s, the Protestant monarchomachists had argued for a universal right of "reaction" against an unjust prince, and they sought a kind of paradigm in the Medieval Germanic feudal relations capable in principle of termination on the same lines as a contract. The English *Magna Carta* and the Danish coronation charter from the 1200s follow the same line of thinking. The theory of a "law of reaction" survived in various versions and was introduced into the new German *Grundgesetz* after the war as authority for a refusal to carry out unlawful orders.

This concept has recently become topical in the Danish debate, following attempts to charge high ranking civil servants with failing to refuse to carry out "unlawful" decisions. Facing this we have the civil servants' duty of loyalty and obedience, a duty which is important in a political system which does not distinguish between administrative and political service. A civil servant will therefore only be able to refuse to carry out "clearly unlawful" orders.

Otherwise, the "law of reaction" has no greater legal substance than the "civil disobedience" developed by the American Henry David Thoreau (1817-62) during the last century, and which was claimed by Marcuse in the 70s as a "legal" justification for not following rules one did not like.

The theory of natural law was generally rejected by the critical philosophy and the historical school of thought in the late 1700s and early 1800s. Positive law as a "natural history" phenomenon or codification theory dominated throughout the industrial period of the nineteenth century. The minimal state favoured free will and free competition. With democracy and recognition of human rights, the need for natural law and a law of reaction is less.

In more recent times we have seen examples of ethical theories of law of various kinds which are not concerned merely with establishing the authority of law in superordinate non-human powers. In other words, natural law theory is involving itself in issues other than that of the law's formal *validity*. It is also interested in the *content* of the law, the substantive natural law and the issue of its *specification*, i.e. the application of the rule in cases of doubt. The first question concerns the law's moral content: are the rules of law invalid if in conflict with morality? In Catholic countries and in accordance with Catholic moral philosophy, neo-Thomist natural law has argued that rules of law which are in conflict with the moral teachings of the Church are invalid. In recent German theory the formerly positivist-inclined Gustav Radbruch (1878-1949) has written in the postwar period about the Third Reich that it was *"Unrecht als System"*.

With a basis in phenomenological philosophy, others have established a "substantive hierarchy of values" and argued in favour of an "a priori" natural law theory capable of invalidating a legal system which does not recognise this intuitively grounded value system (Alois Troller, Helmut Coing). Their thoughts carry some relation to a neo-Kantian relative natural law theory (A. Verdross) which recognises that the natural law concept has a logical structure, but varying content depending on the cultural situation. Another Kantian variation of the German science of law (the Marburger school) placed emphasis on justice as the idea which the law should strive to realise.

The third natural law problem, the *specification problem*, has taken its starting point in the *"nature of things"*, as the key to a logical solution to a concrete case. In its modern form, the term goes back to Montesquieu's relative natural law theory, which claimed that the law is eternal and immutable, but that it was nevertheless dependent on people's habits and external circumstances. Montesquieu did, however, take it for granted that there was a "necessary connection", *rapport necessaire*, between law and society, and that this necessary connection made it possible with the aid of reason to find the right solution to practical problems. The tool was *"nature des choses"*, in later German theory *"Natur der Sache"*, which reflects the idealistic philosophy's attempts at establishing a connection between norm and reality. In Kantian theory this attempt was based on the proposition that the human mind is capable of projection on to the external world, and in Hegelian theory on the proposition that the external world is structured logically. Both variations thus found the relationship between knowledge and the external world, between norm and reality, unproblematic. The gap between knowledge and value judgements was bridged by reducing it to a "formulation" in language of the factual circumstances of the specific situation.

In Denmark, A.S. Ørsted (1778-1860) tied his "realist theory of law" to Montesquieu's concepts of interpretation, *esprit de lois*, or the spirit of the law, and *nature des choses*, or the nature of things. Using this practical concept, which refers to ordinary common sense, Ørsted succeeded in establishing an independent realist theory of law based on the interaction of the study and the practice of law, including the publication for the first time of systematic law reports.

In more recent schools of thought, attempts have been made to establish a theory of substantive natural law. In his criticism of Scandinavian realism, the Norwegian Frede Castberg (1893-1977) has demanded that the legal system respect human rights and the concept of "justice", although the concept is not defined any further than that. As we have seen, the American Lon Fuller has similarly pointed to the ethical requirements of the legal system, but like Hart's "minimum content", they appear to be conditions of efficacy rather than conditions of validity. They are ethical demands standing in the same relation to the legal system as K.E. Løgstrup's (1905-81) "spontaneous expressions of life" do to ethics.

Natural law and justice are thus expressions of the demands of ethics on the law, but they are different demands. Natural law theory has been especially concerned with the question of validity, while justice theory has been concerned rather with content and procedure. The demand for justice is, however, a demand with a certain structure, namely the different types of equality, while morality can make other and more diffuse demands on the content of the law.

ABUSE OF THE LAW

The difference between morality and moralism is the way in which morality is used in argumentation. A moral argument is one where morality is used as basis for a decision, while a moralistic argument uses morality as a pretext to gain a result desired for other reasons.

A moralistic argument is thus an unjust argument, as no real balance exists between argument and motive, in the same way as "abuse of power" constitutes an invalid argument under administrative law, when the administration uses an administrative procedure to gain an administrative end which was not intended by the rule or suited for the purpose.

Abuse of power can also occur in private law, if a person exploits a position in law to gain an unjust advantage for himself or others. This element of arbitrariness, which could arise if a person was able to decide independently which of several persons should carry a loss, is normally eliminated through a general principle of proportionate cover of loss between several tortfeasors through rules of regress and rules of limitations in the right to choose, e.g. in connection with payment when several obligations have been entered into. Legal abuse can occur in several other ways and may ultimately be stopped by a no-harassment rule which expresses the common dictum of justice that no false weights may be placed in *Lady Justitia*'s scales.

It would also run counter to the general principle of equality if a person could be bound by a "lopsided legal matter", i.e. that one of the parties was bound, but the other party in a mutual legal matter was not. The promisor is therefore only bound for a brief period, the time limit set for acceptance of the offer, until the promisee has had an opportunity to decide whether he wants to accept the offer. If he does not, the offer will lapse (Danish Contract Act, Section 3). This means that the other party to a legal agreement will be released if the first party's obligations become invalid or lapse (cf. Danish Act on Legal Capacity Section 43, on invalidity of promises given by minors in mutual agreements).

PRIORITY

In Medieval English contract law the principle of "consideration" was developed, under which, apart from sealed documents, a party was bound and only bound if he had received an advantage or incurred a disadvantage of a financial kind, *quid pro quo*. In English contract law, the principle has never been that one was bound because a promise had been given, but because a deal had been concluded.

Another principle (production/accretion) has been that the person performing a task is also as a rule the owner of the task. John Locke applied this principle in arguing for property rights, as the person who has tilled a piece of land must also have a claim to its harvest, that is to say to retain control of the land. It is generally recognised that land rights are of no interest to hunter-gatherers, and that "property rights" and rights of succession only became a legal necessity with farming, where values accumulated in the form of tilled land, livestock and stationary buildings.

In hunter-gatherer cultures a need already exists, however, to establish rules governing rights of priority in case of conflicts of interest among several competitors, and here too it was the first person on the spot who had first right. The hunter who tracks and kills the prey is also entitled to it. In the old Greenland sealer and hunter society it was, as far as I know, the hunter who first saw the prey who had the right to it.

The rule of priority and the rule of property rights must thus also be seen in light of the principle of justice, while the latter has also had a practical function in preventing conflict, as does the principle of possession. The general burden of proof which dictates that the person wanting to change the state of affairs must be able to give grounds for the change should be seen in this light.

CONCLUSIONS

The conclusion must be that justice is a concept linked with primary human value judgements and basic social needs for order.

Justice is a moral concept which acquires an independent meaning in law for the very reason that law moves from its status of divine custom in primitive society to becoming a social means of control. While, in the old society, law and justice are two sides of the same coin, justice in the new society however becomes a moral demand concerning the content of the law and its administration.

Justice is no ordinary or unstructured moral demand concerning the law. In all its meanings, it refers to equality in one sense or another. Equality is not, however, a simple concept, as various considerations and criteria may enter into the comparison.

In its original sense, justice refers to equal weight: service for service, eye for eye. From time immemorial, the scales have been the symbol of the law. Man must get his just desserts both in life and death. That is corrective justice.

In the urban society, a new form of justice is needed. This is distributive justice based on each person's social merit. Taken to its extremes, this line of thought leads to a utilitarian or socialist view of society, depending on whether freedom or equality is adopted as the highest value.

The concept of justice contains a formal core, namely that like cases must be treated alike. In this sense it is identical to the demand that the law must be expressed in rules in contrast to arbitrary commands.

The concept of justice has a static content, at least in so far as its substantive content changes with social culture.

The western European concept of justice was developed in association with Renaissance individualism, which considered the individual person the smallest social unit and the holder of rights. These rights protect the freedom and integrity of the individual, partly against the equal right of freedom of other individuals and partly against infringements by society.

The substantive law principles underpinning the individual components of the legal system are not merely political or merely moral principles, but the basis of legal argumentation with roots in material justice.

This concept of rights means that its delimitations cannot be fixed by administrative procedures, but only by judicial procedures in accordance with general procedural principles.

Procedural justice reflects the principle of the impartial and "objective" decision in respect of the decision-maker and the arguments which may be accepted as "true weights" on the scales. The arguments must not only constitute valid norms, but must also be used as grounds and not as pretexts for the decision.

Abuse of the law and harassment are examples of partial application of law and rights. The principle of priority (first in time and first in right) is linked with the concept of justice of acquisition and payment, just as property rights, the principle of possession and mutuality are linked in contract law.

Rules must not only be applied equally, they must also be enforced justly, as no-one will tolerate a restriction in their freedom of action unless the same restriction applies to others as well.

The rules must be used in connection with concrete situations, and this gives scope for the justice requirement called equity. It developed from the Greek *epieikeia* and the Roman *aequitas*, which means that the rule must be applied in equal measure, but that consideration must also be given to the actual circumstances (the nature of the matter).

In recent language philosophy, this principle has found support in the principle that an actual situation cannot be described objectively, but only through interpretative comparison of the relevant rule with its socio-typical control model. The rule is a language generalisation on the basis of the typical situation at which the rule is aimed, and its application therefore requires not only a language but also a teleological (purpose) and pragmatic (effect) interpretation.

Justice is thus not the same as natural law, although both concepts concern the demands of morality on the law and originate in the separation of law from ethics. Justice is set apart by its special structure of equality and comparative process, while natural law is set apart by its concern for the authority of the law, its validity and the duty of obedience of individual people (law of reaction, civil disobedience).

Similarly to legal arguments, justice arguments look backward towards an existing duty, but while legal arguments are normative in the sense that they refer to legal norms, justice arguments are first and foremost oriented towards primary value judgements, albeit with some structure.

One particular question is how duty arguments can appear convincing compared with purpose-oriented arguments. How can the reference to a duty be more convincing than references to an advantage? The element of sanctions is of course important, so transgressions of legal rules must be sanctioned.

But apart from sanctions, the duty argument can carry conviction if one may trust that an immediate advantage will be replaced by a (greater) future advantage. An organised society cannot exist without regulation by law, and the moral duty to obey the law is a necessary replacement of the instincts which ensure the functioning of a small society.

Logical empiricism's criticism of the concept of justice was not adequate. It posited partly that concepts are meaningful only if they have an external component (semantic reference), partly that it is possible to describe this external world objectively. If both propositions are rejected, this criticism dissolves, and this is exactly what happens when the hermeneutic language analysis is applied.

It is a fact that recent legal practice has torn itself free of the "realist" school of thought, having apparently realised a need to be able to express its instinctive value judgements in the form of "fairness" and "equity", even where the legal source materials do not refer explicitly to justice.

REFERENCES

I. Own Works

A. Books and Monographs

Fire obligationsretlige afhandlinger, Copenhagen 1965 (reprinted 1987, 1989).

Træk af privatrettens udvikling og systematik + Systematik, begreber, metode. *Acta Jutlandica* XXXVIII:I, Social Science Series 12, Aarhus 1966 (also in *Tidsskrift for rettsvitenskap* 1966, 584 and *Vertrag und Recht*, 1968: "Entwicklung und Methode des Privatrechts").

Skyld og ansvar. Ed. Stig Jørgensen ... [et al.], Copenhagen 1967.

Vertrag und Recht, Copenhagen 1968.

Ret og samfund, Copenhagen 1970 (reprinted 1989).

Law and Society, Aarhus 1971.

Erstatning for personskade og tab af forsørger, 3rd ed., Copenhagen 1972.

Lovmål og dom, Copenhagen 1975.

Values in Law: Ideas, Principles and Rules, Copenhagen 1978.

Ethik und Gerechtigkeit: zwei historisch-rechtstheoretische Vorlesungen, Göttingen 1980.

Pluralis Juris: Towards a Relativistic Theory of Law. *Acta Jutlandica* XLVI, Social Science Series 14, Aarhus 1982.

Reason and Reality. *Acta Jutlandica* LXII, Social Science Series 17, Aarhus 1986.

Danmarks kongemagt og dens fødsel, Aarhus 1987.

Fragments of Legal Cognition, Aarhus 1988.

B. Articles

"Kausalitetsspørgsmål i erstatningsretten", *Ugeskrift for Retsvæsen* 1953B, 33-49 and 225-28.

"Årsagsproblemer i forbindelse med personskade", *Nordisk Forsikrings Tidsskrift*, vol. 40, 1960, 185-99.

"Skærpet erstatningsansvar", *Ugeskrift for Retsvæsen* 1961B, 81-96 (also in *Scandinavian Studies in Law*, vol. 7, 1963, 25-59: "Towards Strict Liability in Tort".

"Spredte bemærkninger om adækvans", *Juristen* 1961, 195-206.

"Naturaleksekution", *Ugeskrift for Retsvæsen* 1962B, 165-79 (also in *Fire obligationsretlige afhandlinger*, 1965 (see Books and Monographs)).

"Forudsætning og mangel", *Ugeskrift for Retsvæsen* 1963B, 157-76 (also in *Fire obligationsretlige afhandlinger*, 1965 (see Books and Monographs)).

"Aftalelov og acceptfrist", *Ugeskrift for Retsvæsen* 1963B, 285-99 (also in *Fire obligationsretlige afhandlinger*, 1965 (see Books and Monographs)).

"Erstatningsrettens udvikling", *Juristen* 1963, 301-10.

"Misligholdelse", *Tidsskrift for rettsvitenskap* 1964, 449-503 (also in *Fire obligationsretlige afhandlinger*, 1965 (see Books and Monographs)).

"Aftalen som form", *Tidsskrift for rettsvitenskap* 1965, 400-31 (also in *Scandinavian Studies in Law*, vol. 10, 1966, 97-125: "Contract as Form", in *Vertrag und Recht*, 1968 (see Books and Monographs): "Der Vertrag als Form").

"Træk af de retlige ideers historie i komparativ belysning", *Ugeskrift for Retsvæsen* 1967B, 153-64 (also in *Vertrag und Recht*, 1968 (see Books and Monographs): "Auszüge aus der Geschichte der rechtlichen Ideen in komparativer Beleuchtung").

"Grotius' kontraktslære", *Tidsskrift for rettsvitenskap* 1967, 457-73 (also in *Vertrag und Recht*, 1968 (see Books and Monographs): "Die Lehre des Grotius vom Vertrag", in *Scandinavian Studies in Law*, vol. 13, 1969, 107-25: "Grotius' Doctrine of Contract", and in *Values in Law*, 1978 (see Books and Monographs)).

"Fuldmagtsproblemer", *Juristen* 1968, 401-29.

"Rudolf v. Jhering og nordisk retsvidenskab", *Ugeskrift for Retsvæsen* 1968B, 245-49 (also in *Jherings Erbe, Göttinger Symposion...*, 1970: "Die Bedeutung Jherings für die neuere skandinavische Rechtslehre", and in *Lovmål og dom*, 1975 (see Books and Monographs)).

"Erstatning og forsikring", *Nordisk Forsikrings Tidsskrift*, vol. 49, 1969, 15-36.

"Argumentation and Decision", *Festskrift til Alf Ross*, eds. Mogens Blegvad ... [et al.], Copenhagen 1969, 261-84 (also in *Lovmål og dom*, 1975 and in *Values in Law*, 1978 (see Books and Monographs)).

"Typologi og realisme", *Nordisk gjenklang: Festskrift til Carl Jacob Arnholm*, Oslo 1969, 143-63 (also in *Nachrichten der Akademie der Wissenschaften in Göttingen*, 1971: "Typologie und Realismus", and in *Lovmål og dom*, 1975 (see Books and Monographs)).

154   *References*

"Grundzüge der Entwicklung der skandinavischen Rechtswissenschaft", *Juristenzeitung* 1970, 529-35.
"Modstandsret og ungdomsoprør", *Tidsskrift for rettsvitenskap* 1970, 198-208.
"Norm og virkelighed", *Tidsskrift for rettsvitenskap* 1970, 484-503 (also in *Rechtstheorie*, vol. 2, 1971, 1-16: "Norm und Wirklichkeit", and in *Lovmål og dom*, 1975 (see Books and Monographs)).
"Grundtræk af de danske retskilders historie", *Tidsskrift for rettsvitenskap* 1971, 201-10 (also in *Revue internationale de droit comparé*, vol. 23, 1971, 65-75: "Les traits principaux de l'évolution des sources du droit danois").
"Die rechtliche Lage des Menschen in einem ständig wechselnden gesellschaftlichen Modell", *Österreichische Zeitschrift für Öffentliches Recht*, vol. 23, 1972, 213-28.
"Ideologi og retsvidenskab", *Juristen* 1973, 180-91 (also in *Det lærde Selskabs Publikationsserie* 1973, No. 3, in *Scandinavian Studies in Law*, vol. 18, 1974, 87-107: "Ideology and Science", in *Lovmål og dom*, 1975, and in *Values in Law*, 1978 (see Books and Monographs)).
"Hermeneutik og fortolkning", *Tidsskrift for rettsvitenskap* 1973, 626-36 (also in *Lovmål og dom*, 1975 (see Books and Monographs)).
"Symmetri og retfærdighed", *Det lærde Selskabs Publikationsserie* (New Series), Aarhus 1975, 7-8, pp. 50 ff. (also in *Estudios de Filosofia del Derecho y Ciencia Juridica: en Memoria y Homenaje al Catedrático Don Luis Legaz y Lacambra*, vol. 1, Madrid 1977, 623-44: "Symmetrie und Gerechtigkeit", in *Ethik und Gerechtigkeit*, 1980 (see Books and Monographs), in *Lovmål og dom*, 1975 (see Books and Monographs), and in *Values in Law*, 1978 (see Books and Monographs): "Symmetry and Justice").
"En modern samhällsfilosofi", *Svensk Tidskrift*, vol. 63, 1976, 238-45 (also in *Udfordringer*, Aarhus 1976).
"Idealisme og realisme i retslæren", *Tidskrift utgiven av Juridiska Föreningen i Finland* 1976, vol. 112, 3-29.
"Retspositivisme og naturret", *Acta Jutlandica* XLVI, Samfunds-videnskabelig Serie 13, Aarhus 1977.
"Naturret i nutiden", *Uppsalaskolan och efteråt. Rättsfilosofiskt symposium, Uppsala 23-26 maj 1977*, Uppsala 1978, 53-62 (also in *Values in Law*, 1978 (see Books and Monographs): "Natural Law Today").
"Ejendomsrettens begreb", *Festskrift till Per Stjernquist*, Lund 1978, 29-42.
"Abuse of Rights According to Nordic Law", *L'abus de droit. Inchieste di diritto comparato*, ed. M. Rotondi, Padova 1979, vol. 7, 197-209.

"Doctrines in Strict Law in Scandinavia (Comparative Legal Doctrines)", *The Unity of Strict Law: A Comparative Study*, ed. Ralph A. Newman, Brussels 1978, 199-214.

"Retsafgørelsen og dens begrundelse", *Tidskrift utgiven av Juridiska Föreningen i Finland*, vol. 115, 1979, 318-38.

"Über die allgemeine Rechtslehre in Dänemark", *Archiv für Rechts- und Sozialphilosophie*, Beiheft N.F. 13, 1980, 25-33.

"Demokratie und Völkerbewegung", *Filosofia del Derecho y Filosofia Politica*, vol. II, Mexico 1981, 83-105.

"Johs. Andenæs og almenpræventionen", *Lov og frihet: Festskrift til Johs. Andenæs*, eds. Anders Bratholm, Nils Christie, Torkel Opsahl, Oslo 1982, 177-84.

"Does Reality Exist?", *Festschrift für Karl Larenz*, eds. Claus-Wilhelm Canaris, Uwe Diederichsen, München 1983, 291-301 (also in *Reason and Reality*, 1986 (see Books and Monographs)).

"Pluralis Juris", *Archiv für Rechts- und Sozialphilosophie*, Beiheft 20, 13-19 (also in *Theory of Legal Science*, eds. Aleksander Peczenik, Lars Lindahl, and Bert van Roermund, Dordrecht 1984, and *Reason and Reality*, 1986 (see Books and Monographs)).

"Moral und Effektivität", *Theorie der Normen* — *Festgabe für Ota Weinberger*, eds. Werner Krawietz ...[et al.], Berlin 1984, 119-35 (also in *Reason and Reality*, 1986 (see Books and Monographs): "Effectiveness and Morality").

"Grundnorm und Paradox", *Rechtstheorie*, Beiheft 5, 1984, 179-91 (also in *Reason and Reality*, 1986 (see Books and Monographs): "Basic Norm and Paradox").

"Contract as a Social Form of Life", *Rechtstheorie*, vol. 16, 1985, 201-16 (also in *Reason and Reality*, 1986 (see Books and Monographs)).

"Kvalitetskriterier i retsvidenskaben", *Arbejdsretligt tidsskrift* 1985, 246-50.

"Status og kontrakt som model for samfundets organisation", *Skabelse, udvikling, samfund: en forelæsningsrække*, Det lærde Selskab, *Acta Jutlandica* LX, Samfundsvidenskabelig Serie 16, Aarhus 1985, 163-74.

"Versuche dezentraler Steuerung in Skandinavien", *Steuerungsprobleme in Skandinavien (HiMoN-DB)*. Beitrag zu dem internationalen Symposion "Grenzen des Rechts. Limitations of Law", Bielefeld 1985, 23-37.

"Demokratiets dilemma", *Samfunn, rett, rettferdighet: Festskrift til Torstein Eckhoff*, eds. Anders Bratholm, Torkel Opsahl, Magnus Aarbakke, Oslo 1986, 402-16 (also in *Reason and Reality*, 1986 (see Books and Monographs): "The Crisis of Democracy").

"Erstatning og udvikling", *Svensk Juristtidning* 1986, 477-88.

"Scandinavian Legal Philosophy", *Rechtstheorie*, Beiheft 9, 289-304 (also in *Reason and Reality*, 1986 (see Books and Monographs)).

"What is Law?", *Legal Pluralism*, eds. Peter Sack and Elisabeth Minchin, Canberra, 1986, 17-31 (also in *Reason and Reality*, 1986 (see Books and Monographs)).

"Ret og religion", *Lov, dom og bok: Festskrift til Sjur Brækhus*, ed. Thor Falkanger, Oslo 1988, 269-75.

"Individual Rights and Contract: Freedom and Reciprocity in Contract law", *Washington University Law Quarterly*, vol. 65, 1987, 722-31.

"Philosophy of Life and Ideology: Who are We?", Festschrift in Honor of Edgar Bodenheimer, *U.C. Davis Law Review*, vol. 21, 1988, 989-99.

"Rettens grænser", *Juristen* 1988, 350-56.

"Retsdogmatikkens tilstand", *Juristen* 1989, 196-202.

"The Limits of Law", *Rechtstheorie*, Beiheft 11, 1990, 23-41.

"Fragment und Ganzheit in der juristischen Methode", *Rechtsdogmatik und praktische Vernunft: Symposion zum 80. Geburtstag von Franz Wieacker*, eds. O. Behrends, M. Diesselhorst, R. Dreier, Göttingen 1990, 57-68.

"Grenzen des Rechts: vom Aufstieg und Verfall des Rechts als Steuerungsmittel". *Rechtstheorie*, vol. 20, 1989, 493-500.

"Jydske Lov i europæisk sammenhæng", *Jydske Lov 750 år*, eds. Ole Fenger and Chr. R. Jansen, Viborg 1991, 18-25.

"Einleitende Bemerkungen zur Ringvorlesung Recht und Rechtslehre im Nationalsozialismus", Kiel 1990. *Recht und Rechtslehre im Nationalsozialismus*, ed. Franz Jürgen Säcker, Kiel 1992, 255-58.

"The State of Legal Dogmatics", *Sprache, Performanz und Ontologie des Rechts: Festgabe für K. Opalek*, eds. W. Krawietz and J. Wróblewski, Berlin 1993, 35-44.

"'Rechtfertigkeit' und Gerechtigkeit: Erkenntnis, Auslegung, Beschreibung", *Rechtsnorm und Rechtswirklichkeit. Festschrift für Werner Krawietz*, eds. Aulis Arnio ... [et al.], Berlin 1993, 515-28.

"Juristen og retorikken", *Retorik, hvad er det — også?*, *Modersmåls-Selskabets Årbog*, 1994, 47-52.

"Language and Reality", *Man, Law and Medicine. Festschrift in Honour of Jan Broekman*, 1996.

"Juristerne og hermeneutikken", *Philosophia* 1996 (forthcoming).

II. Other References

Aarbakke, M. 1966. "Harmonisering af rettskilder", *Tidsskrift for rettsvitenskap* 501.

Aarnio, Aulis. 1983. *Philosophical Perspectives in Jurisprudence*, Helsinki.

Anners, Erik. 1983. *Den europeiske rettens historie*, Oslo.

Bentzon, Viggo. 1914. *Skøn og Regel*, Copenhagen.

Bjarup, Jes. 1978. *Skandinavischer Realismus*, Freiburg.

Bjarup, Jes. 1982. *Reason, Emotion and the Law: Studies in the Philosophy of Axel Hägerström*, Aarhus.

Bock, Sisela. 1979. *Løgn*, Copenhagen.

Brorly, Erik. 1986. "Retskilderne i praksis", *Justitia* 1986, No. 3.

Castberg, Frede. 1965. *Forelesninger over rettsfilosofi*, Oslo.

Christensen, Bent. 1990. "Domstolene og lovgivningsmagten", *Ugeskrift for Retsvæsen* 1990B, 73.

Christie, Nils. 1978. *Som folk flest*, Oslo.

Coase, R.H. 1960. "The Problem of Social Cost", *Journal of Law and Economics*, 51.

Cohen, Felix S. 1950. "Field Theory and Judicial Logic", *Yale Law Journal*, vol. 59, 238.

Coing, Helmut. 1959. *Die juristischen Auslegungsmethoden und die Lehre der allgemeinen Hermeneutik*, Cologne.

Dalberg-Larsen, J. 1977. *Retsvidenskaben som samfundsvidenskab: Et retsteoretisk tema i historisk og aktuel belysning*, Copenhagen.

Dalberg-Larsen, J. 1990. *Lovene og livet: En retssociologisk grundbog*, Copenhagen.

Dreier, Ralf, and Wolfgang Sellert (eds.). 1989. *Recht und Justiz im "Dritten Reich"*, Frankfurt a.M.

Dworkin, Ronald. 1986. *Law's Empire*, London.

Eckhoff, Torstein. 1953. *Rettsvesen og rettsvitenskap i U.S.A.*, Oslo.

Eckhoff, Torstein. 1971. *Rettferdighet ved utveksling og fordeling av verdier*, Oslo.

Eckhoff, Torstein. 1971. *Rettskildelære*, Oslo.

Eckhoff, Torstein & Nils Kristian Sundby. 1976. *Rettssystemer: Systemteoretisk innføring i rettsfilosofien*, Oslo.

Engisch, Karl. 1968. *Die Idee der Konkretisierung: In Recht und Rechtswissenschaft unserer Zeit*, 2nd ed., Heidelberg.

Esser, Josef. 1956. *Grundsatz und Norm in der richterlichen Fortbildung des Rechts: Rechtsvergleichende Beiträge zur Rechtsquellen- und Interpretationslehre*, Tübingen.

Esser, Josef. 1970. *Vorverständnis und Methodenwahl in der Rechtsfindung: Rationalitätsgarantien der richterlichen Entscheidungspraxis*, Frankfurt a.M.

Eyben, W.E. von. 1950. *Strafudmåling: Lovens rammer og dommerens udfyldning*, Copenhagen.

Eyben, W.E. von. 1986. *Bevis*, Copenhagen.

Eyben, W.E. von. 1988. *Juridisk Grundbog 1, Retskilderne*, 4th ed., Copenhagen.

Fenger, Ole. 1971. *Fejde og mandebod: Studier over slægtsansvaret i germansk og gammeldansk ret*, Copenhagen.

Fenger, Ole. 1977. *Romerret i Norden*, Copenhagen.

From, Franz. 1953. *Om oplevelsen af andres adfærd: Et bidrag til den menneskelige adfærds fænomenologi*, Copenhagen.

Fuller, Lon. 1969. *The Morality of Law*, 2nd ed., New Haven.

Gadamer, H.G. 1965. *Wahrheit und Methode: Grundzügen einer philosophischen Hermeneutik*, 2nd ed., Tübingen.

Habermas, Jürgen. 1979. *Erkenntnis und Interesse*, 5th ed., Frankfurt a.M.

Habermas, Jürgen. 1984. *Vorstudien und Ergänzungen zur Theorie des kommunikativen Handelns*, Frankfurt a.M.

Hammershaimb, E. 1966. *Some Aspects of Old Testament Prophecy from Isaiah to Malachi*, Copenhagen.

Hart, H.L.A. & A.M. Honoré. 1959. *Causation in the Law*, Oxford.

Hart, H.L.A. 1994. *The Concept of Law*, 2nd ed., Oxford.

Hayek, F.A. 1982. *Law, Legislation and Liberty: A New Statement of the Liberal Principles of Justice and Political Economy*, London.

Hellner, Jan. 1988. *Rättsteori: En introduktion*, Stockholm.

Illum, Knud. 1945. *Lov og Ret*, Copenhagen.

Kaufmann, A. 1990. *Rechtswissenschaft in der Nach-Neuzeit*, Cologne.

Kelsen, Hans. 1945. *General Theory of Law and State*, Cambridge.

Krawietz, W. 1978. *Juristische Entscheidung und wissenschaftliche Erkenntnis*, Vienna.

Kriele, Martin. 1967. *Theorie der Rechtsgewinnung entwickelt am Problem der Verfassungsinterpretation*, Berlin.

Kruse, Fr. Vinding. 1943. *Retslæren I-II*, Copenhagen.

Kuhn, Thomas. 1970. *The Structure of Scientific Revolution*, 2nd ed., Chicago.

Larenz, Karl. 1991. *Methodenlehre der Rechtswissenschaft*, 6th ed., Berlin.

Lauridsen, P. Stuer. 1974. *Studier i retspolitisk argumentation*, Copenhagen.

Lauridsen, P. Stuer. 1977. *Retslæren*, Copenhagen.

Luhmann, Niklas. 1969. *Legitimation durch Verfahren*, Neuwied am Rhein.

Løgstrup, K.E. 1956. *Den etiske fordring*, Copenhagen.

MacCormick, Neil & Ota Weinberger. 1986. *An Institutional Theory of Law*, Dordrecht.

McBride, William Leon. 1968. "The Essential Role of Models and Analogies in the Philosophy of Law", *New York University Law Review*, vol. 43, 53.

Makkonen, Kaarle. 1965. *Zur Problematik der juristischen Entscheidung: Eine strukturanalytische Studie*, Turku.

Nozick, Robert. 1980. *Anarchy, State and Utopia*, Oxford.

Nørgaard, C.A. & J. Garde. 1988. *Forvaltningsret, sagsbehandling*, 3rd ed., Aarhus.

Olivecrona, Karl. 1971. *Law as Fact*, 2nd ed., London.

Ørsted, A.S. 1822-35. *Haandbog over den danske og norske Lovkyndighed*, Copenhagen.

Perelmann, Chaim. 1963. *Justice et Raison*, Brussels.

Posner, Richard. 1986. *Economic Analysis of Law*, 3rd ed., Boston.

Rasmussen, Erik. 1981. *Lighedsbegreber*, Copenhagen.

Rawls, John. 1971. *A Theory of Justice*, Cambridge, Mass.

Rheinstein, Max. 1970. "Die Rechtshonoratioren und ihr Einfluss auf Charakter und Funktion der Rechtsordnungen", *Rabels Zeitschrift für ausländisches und internationales Privatrecht*, vol. 34, 1.

Ross, Alf. 1953. *Om Ret og Retfærdighed*. English ed. *On Law and Justice*, Cambridge, Mass. 1968.

Ross, Alf. 1974. *Forbrydelse og straf: Analytiske og reformatoriske bidrag til kriminalretten*, Copenhagen.

Rüthers, Bernd. 1968. *Die unbegrenzte Auslegung: Zum Wandel der Privatrechtsordnung im Nationalsozialismus*, Tübingen.

Rønsholdt, Steen. 1987. *Om saglig kommunalforvaltning og kommunal-bestyrelsesmedlemmers inhabilitet*, Copenhagen.

Sandvik, Gudmund. 1989. "Europeisk rettshistorie i mellomalderen", *Jussens Venner*, no. 6-7.

Smith, Adam. 1776. *An Inquiry into the Nature and Causes of the Wealth of Nations*.

Stein, Peter & John Shand. 1974. *Legal Values in Western Society*, Edinburgh.

Strömholm, Stig. 1992. *Rätt, rättskällor och rättstillämpning: En lärobok i allmän rättslära*, 4th ed., Stockholm.

Strömholm, Stig. 1985. *A Short History of Legal Thinking in the West*, Stockholm.

Teubner, Gunther. 1983. "Substantive and Reflexive Elements in Modern Law", *Law and Society Law Review*, vol. 17, 239.

Troller, Alois. 1965. *Überall gültige Prinzipien der Rechtswissenschaft*, Frankfurt a.M.

Verdross, Alfred. 1971. *Statisches und dynamisches Naturrecht*, Freiburg.

Viehweg, Theodor. 1965. *Topik und Jurisprudenz*, 3rd ed., Munich.

Wanscher, Torben. 1979. *Forsamlingsfriheden og "Fælledslaget": Studier til belysning af statens fastlæggelse af grænserne for arbejderbevægelsens forsamlingsfrihed 1872-1874*, Aarhus.

Wesel, Uwe. 1985. *Frühformen des Rechts in vorstaatlichen Gesellschaften*, Frankfurt a.M.

Westermarck, Edward. 1906-08. *The Origin and Development of Moral Ideas*.

Wieacker, Franz. 1967. *Privatrechtsgeschichte der Neuzeit*, 2nd ed., Göttingen.

Wieacker, Franz. 1985. *Voraussetzungen europäischer Rechtskultur*, Göttingen.

Wittgenstein, Ludwig. 1953. *Philosophical Investigations*.

Wittgenstein, Ludwig. 1922. *Tractatus Logico-Philosophicus*.

INDEX

Aagesen, A. *43*
Abraham *127*
Achilles *59*
Adorno, Th. *28*
Aeschylus *59, 122*
Anaximander *15*
Antigone *121-22*
Aquinas, Thomas *61, 97, 142, 144*
Aristotle *15-16, 21, 58-59, 61-63, 72, 75-76, 94, 96-97, 103, 111, 118, 127, 140-41*
Augustine *60, 76, 96-97, 117, 142*
Austin, J.L. *30*
Bentzon, Viggo *43*
Bergson, Henri *24*
Bock, Sisela *104*
Bodin, J. *62, 142*
Brentano, Franz v. *24*
Baat *126*
Caesar *112*
Calvin, Jean *76*
Castberg, Frede *145*
Chomsky, Noam *46*
Christian IV *116, 129*
Christian V *97*
Christie, Nils *119*
Cicero *117*
Coing, Helmut *144*
Copernicus, Nicholas *62*
Demosthenes *118*
Descartes, René *17, 22*
Dewey, T. *38*
Dice *59, 127*

Dilthey, Wilhelm *17, 29*
Draco *57*
Dumas, Alexander *121*
Dworkin, Ronald *66, 101, 108-9*
Evaldsen, A.C. *43*
Ewald, Carl *124*
Ezekiel *116*
Falkberget, Johan *129*
Fichte, J.G. *24, 29*
Frank, Jerome *38*
From, Franz *48, 103*
Fuller, Lon *77, 95, 103, 108, 145*
Gelasius *60*
Grammaticus, Saxo *130*
Grotius, Hugo *27, 62-63, 76, 142-43*
Habermas, Jürgen *27, 66, 68, 78, 114*
Hammershaimb, E. *124*
Hart, H.L.A. *39-40, 77, 101, 104-6, 108-9, 145*
Hayek, F.A. *115*
Hector *59*
Hegel, G.W.F. *23, 144*
Heidegger, Martin *26, 29*
Hobbes, Thomas *63, 76, 97, 142-43*
Holmes, Oliver Wendell *38*
Homer *57*
Honoré, A.M. *39*
Hume, David *22, 77, 128*
Husserl, Edmund *24*
Hägerström, Axel *25, 30*
Illum, Knud *36, 41, 43, 131*
James, William *25, 38*

Jhering, Rudolph v. *34, 65*
Kampmann, Viggo *114*
Kant, Immanuel *22-23, 50, 65,
    77, 93, 99, 115, 144*
Kelsen, Hans *39-40, 105-6, 109*
Kepler *62*
Kidnar, Richard *35*
Kruse, Frederik Vinding *33,
    107*
Lassen, Julius *43*
Laxness, Halldor *121*
Locke, John *63, 130, 148*
Luhmann, Niklas *66*
Lundstedt, Vilh. *33*
Luther, Martin *76*
Løgstrup, K.E. *145*
MacCormick, N. *27, 66*
Marchiavelli, Niccolo *97*
Marcuse, Herbert *143*
Marsilius of Padua *62, 142*
Marx, Karl *78, 97, 113*
Montesquieu, Charles *64, 130,
    144-45*
Moore, G.E. *24, 29*
Moses *57*
Napoleon *63*
Ørsted, A.S. *43, 64, 145*
Pericles *118*
Piaget, J. *46*
Piso *116*
Plato *15, 21, 59, 74, 94, 103,
    140-41*
Poulsen, Henrik *116*
Pufendorf, S. *63, 76*
Pythagoras *15, 127*

Radbruch, Gustav *106, 144*
Rasmussen, Erik *113*
Rawls, L. *27, 114*
Ross, Alf *5, 12, 30, 33, 38-45,
    83, 106-7, 119*
Rousseau, J.-J. *63*
Russell, Bertrand *30*
Rønsholdt, Steen *134*
Savigny, Carl von *49, 63-65*
Shakespeare, William *121*
Smith, Adam *79, 128*
Socrates *103, 130, 140*
Solomon *116*
Solon *58*
Sophocles *59, 121-22*
Sunesen, Anders *128, 142*
Swift, Jonathan *48*
Tegnér, Esajas *47*
Teubner, Gunther *66, 68, 78*
Thomas Aquinas, *see* Aquinas
Thomasius, C. *63*
Thoreau, Henry David *143*
Thucydides *81, 89, 95-96, 111*
Torp, C. *43*
Troller, Alois *144*
Uffe *130*
Valdemar *67, 96*
Verdross, A. *144*
Wanscher, T. *136*
Weinberger, O. *27, 66*
William of Ockham *21, 62*
Wittgenstein, L. *26, 29*
Wolff, C. *63*
Zoroaster (Zarathustra) *127*